THE DISCIPLE'S PERSONALITY

MasterLife

BOOK 2

Avery T. Willis, Jr.
Kay Moore

LifeWay Press®
Nashville, Tennessee

13th printing 2006

ISBN 0-7673-2580-X

This book is a resource in the Personal Life subject area of the Christian Growth Study Plan.
Course CG-0169

Dewey Decimal Classification: 248.4
Subject Heading: DISCIPLESHIP

Design: Edward Crawford
Cover illustration: Mick Wiggins

To order additional copies of this resource: WRITE LifeWay Church Resources Customer Service, One LifeWay Plaza, Nashville, TN 37234-0113; FAX order to (615) 251-5933; PHONE 1-800-458-2772; E-MAIL *orderentry@lifeway.com*; order ONLINE at *www.lifeway.com*; or visit the LifeWay Christian Store serving you.

Printed in the United States of America

Leadership and Adult Publishing
LifeWay Church Resources
One LifeWay Plaza
Nashville, TN 37234-0175

Contents

The Authors

AVERY T. WILLIS, JR., the author and developer of *MasterLife,* is the former senior vice-president of overseas operations at the International Mission Board of the Southern Baptist Convention. The original *MasterLife: Discipleship Training for Leaders,* published in 1980, has been used by more than 250,000 people in the United States and has been translated into more than 50 different languages for use by untold thousands. Willis is also the author of *Indonesian Revival: Why Two Million Came to Christ, The Biblical Basis of Missions, MasterBuilder: Multiplying Leaders, BibleGuide to Discipleship and Doctrine,* and several books in Indonesian.

Willis served for 10 years as a pastor in Oklahoma and Texas and for 14 years as a missionary to Indonesia, during which he served for 6 years as the president of the Indonesian Baptist Theological Seminary. Before assuming his present position, he served as the director of the Adult Department of the Discipleship and Family Development Division, the Sunday School Board (now LifeWay Christian Resources) of the Southern Baptist Convention, where he introduced the Lay Institute for Equipping (LIFE), a series of in-depth discipleship courses.

KAY MOORE served as the coauthor of this updated edition of *MasterLife.* Formerly a design editor in the Adult Department of the Discipleship and Family Development Division, the Sunday School Board of the Southern Baptist Convention, she led the editorial team that produced the LIFE Support Series, biblically based courses that help people deal with critical issues in their lives. A writer, editor, and conference leader, Moore has authored or coauthored numerous books on family life, relationships, and inspirational topics. She is the author of *Gathering the Missing Pieces in an Adopted Life* and is a frequent contributor to religious magazines and devotional guides.

Introduction

MasterLife is a developmental, small-group discipleship process that will help you develop a lifelong, obedient relationship with Christ. This book, *MasterLife 2: The Disciple's Personality*, is the second of four books in that discipleship process. The other three books are *MasterLife 1: The Disciple's Cross*, *MasterLife 3: The Disciple's Victory*, and *MasterLife 4: The Disciple's Mission*. These studies will enable you to acknowledge Christ as your Master and to master life in Him.

WHAT'S IN IT FOR YOU

The goal of *MasterLife* is your discipleship—for you to become like Christ. To do that, you must follow Jesus, learn to do the things He instructed His followers to do, and help others become His disciples. In these ways *MasterLife* will enable you to discover the satisfaction of following Christ as His disciple and the joy of that relationship with Him. *MasterLife* was designed to help you make the following definition of *discipleship* a way of life:

> Christian discipleship is developing a personal, lifelong, obedient relationship with Jesus Christ in which He transforms your character into Christlikeness; changes your values into Kingdom values; and involves you in His mission in the home, the church, and the world.

In *MasterLife 1: The Disciple's Cross* you explored your personal relationship with Jesus Christ. You learned how to draw the Disciple's Cross to illustrate the balanced life Christ wants His disciples to have. You learned that Christ wants to be at the center of your life so that everything you do is an outgrowth of your relationship with Him.

You will continue to focus on your relationship with Christ in *MasterLife 2: The Disciple's Personality*. However, in this study you will focus on Christ's transforming your character into Christlikeness through the work of the Holy Spirit. Although you are a Christian, you may wonder why you continue to sin despite your best intentions, as if two selves are at war inside you—one controlled by the Spirit and one controlled by the flesh. Jesus' disciples were not Christlike when they were born again, and neither were you. In this study you will learn how the Holy Spirit can change your character and behavior into Christlikeness so that He can work through your will and your life. If you deny yourself and open yourself to the leading of the Holy Spirit, who lives in you, your character can grow more like that of Christ. The outgrowth of having Christ at the center of your personality is life in the Spirit. He will build Christlike character in you as you practice the six disciplines you learned in *MasterLife 1: The Disciple's Cross:*

- Spend time with the Master
- Live in the Word
- Pray in faith
- Fellowship with believers
- Witness to the world
- Minister to others

THE *MASTERLIFE* PROCESS

MasterLife 2: The Disciple's Personality is part of a 24-week discipleship process. Completing all four courses in *MasterLife* will provide you information and experiences you need to be Christ's disciple. Each book builds on the other and is recommended as a prerequisite for the one that follows.

The *MasterLife* process involves six elements. Each element is essential to your study of *MasterLife*.

1. The *daily activities* in this book lead you into a closer walk with Christ. Doing these exercises daily is important.
2. The *weekly assignments* in "My Walk with the Master This Week" are real-life experiences that will change your life.
3. The *leader* is a major element. Discipleship is a relationship. It is not something you do by yourself. You need human models, instruction, and accountability to become what Christ intends for you to be. To become a better disciple, you need a leader to whom you can relate personally and regularly—

someone who can teach you, model behaviors, and hold you accountable.

4. The weekly *group sessions* help you reflect on the concepts and experiences in *MasterLife* and help you apply the ideas to your life. The group sessions allow you to experience the profound changes Christ is making in your life. Each group session also provides training for the next stage of spiritual growth.
5. *Christ* is the Discipler, and you become His disciple. As you fully depend on Him, He works through each of the previous elements and uses them to support you.
6. The body of Christ—the *church*—is vital for complete discipling to take place. You depend on Christian friends for fellowship, strength, and ministry opportunities. Without the church, you lack the support you need to grow in Christ.

HOW TO STUDY THIS BOOK

Each day for five days a week you will be expected to study a segment of the material in this workbook and to complete the related activities. You may need from 20 to 30 minutes of study time each day. Even if you find that you can study the material in less time, spreading the study over five days will give you time to apply the truths to your life.

You will notice that discipline logos appear before various assignments:

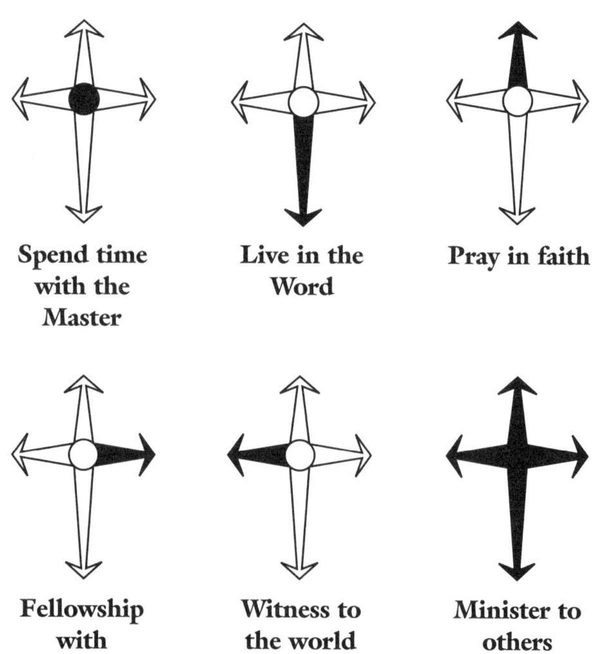

These logos link certain activities to the six disciplines you are learning to incorporate into your life as a disciple. These activities are part of your weekly assignments, which are outlined in "My Walk with the Master This Week" at the beginning of each week's material. The discipline logos differentiate your weekly assignments from the activities related to your study for that particular day.

Set a definite time and select a quiet place to study with little or no interruption. Keep a Bible handy to find Scriptures as directed in the material. Memorizing Scripture is an important part of your work. Set aside a portion of your study period for memory work. Unless I have deliberately chosen another version for a specific emphasis, all Scriptures in *MasterLife* are quoted from the *New International Version* of the Bible. However, feel free to memorize Scripture from any version of the Bible you prefer. I suggest that you write each memory verse on a card that you can review often during the week.

After completing each day's assignments, turn to the beginning of the week's material. If you completed an activity that corresponds to one listed under "My Walk with the Master This Week," place a vertical line in the diamond beside the activity. During the following group session a member of the group will verify your work and will add a horizontal line in the diamond, forming a cross in each diamond. This process will confirm that you have completed each weekly assignment before you continue. You may do the assignments at your own pace, but be sure to complete all of them before the next group session.

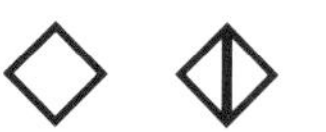

THE DISCIPLE'S PERSONALITY

On pages 133–39 you will find the Disciple's Personality presentation. The Disciple's Personality, which explains how to become more Christlike in character and behavior, will be the focal point for all you learn in this book. Each week you will study an additional portion of the Disciple's Personality and will learn the Scripture that accompanies it. By the end of the study you will be able to explain the Disciple's Personality in your own words and to say all of the verses that go with it.

Discipleship Covenant

To participate in *MasterLife*, you are asked to dedicate yourself to God and to your *MasterLife* group by making the following commitments. You may not currently be able to do everything listed, but by signing this covenant, you pledge to adopt these practices as you progress through the study.

As a disciple of Jesus Christ, I commit myself to—

- acknowledge Jesus Christ as Lord of my life each day;
- attend all group sessions unless providentially hindered;
- spend from 20 to 30 minutes a day as needed to complete all assignments;
- have a daily quiet time;
- keep a Daily Master Communication Guide about the way God speaks to me and I speak to Him;
- be faithful to my church in attendance and stewardship;
- love and encourage each group member;
- share my faith with others;
- keep in confidence anything that others share in the group sessions;
- submit myself to others willingly in accountability;
- become a discipler of others as God gives opportunities;
- support my church financially by practicing biblical giving;
- pray daily for group members.

____________________ ____________________

____________________ ____________________

____________________ ____________________

____________________ ____________________

____________________ ____________________

Signed ______________________________ Date ____________

WEEK 1

Do God's Will

This Week's Goal

You will be able to understand and do God's will as the Holy Spirit works in you.

My Walk with the Master This Week

You will complete the following activities to develop the six biblical disciplines. When you have completed each activity, draw a vertical line in the diamond beside it.

SPEND TIME WITH THE MASTER

◇ Have a quiet time each day, working toward the goal of having quiet times 21 consecutive days. Check the box beside each day you have a quiet time this week: ❑ Sunday ❑ Monday ☑ Tuesday ❑ Wednesday ☑ Thursday ☑ Friday ☑ Saturday

LIVE IN THE WORD

◇ Read your Bible every day. Write what God says to you and what you say to God.

◇ Memorize Philippians 2:13.

PRAY IN FAITH

◇ Pray for non-Christian friends of group members.

◇ Confess your sins to God and accept that God has forgiven you.

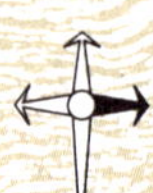

FELLOWSHIP WITH BELIEVERS

◇ Spend time with a member of your family.

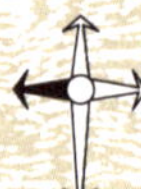

WITNESS TO THE WORLD

◇ Think of five persons to whom you need to witness and write their names on the Prayer-Covenant List. Or make friends with five persons to whom you can witness in the future.

MINISTER TO OTHERS

◇ Learn the Unified Personality and Natural Person parts of the Disciple's Personality.

This Week's Scripture-Memory Verse

"It is God who works in you to will and to act according to his good purpose" (Phil. 2:13).

DAY 1

Who's in Charge?

One day a 16-year-old girl asked me about God's will. I told her that God has a purpose for every person. To make my point, I used several illustrations: "Do you know how many sections are in an orange? An orange usually has 10 sections. A watermelon usually has an even number of stripes. Grains like wheat, barley, millet, and rye have an even number of grains on a stalk. In a fully developed ear of corn an even number of rows are on each ear, an even number of grains are in each row, and an even number of silks are in the tassel." I asked her, "Do you think it's just an accident that so many things God has made have such symmetry?"

She asked, "Does that mean I have to do whatever God wills me to do?" I answered: "No, although God has a perfect will for your life that He wants you to follow, He does not force you to. He leads you to do His will, but He gives you the freedom to make your own choice."

I went on to explain: "It's as if God has a blueprint for your life. Although He may want to build a beautiful mansion from your life, you can still choose to build a shack. But God's intent is that you build according to His will. Make sure that Christ is the foundation of your life. Let the Holy Spirit be the Builder. He can build far better than you can."

I watched to see how God worked in the girl's life. Later she became a pastor's wife, and eventually she and her husband served God as missionaries in a foreign country. She made Christ the foundation and let the Holy Spirit guide her and build her life.

In the account you read, what was the key to this young woman's finding God's will in her life?

Making Christ the foundation
yielding to his instructions

The key to finding God's will was making Christ the foundation and allowing the Holy Spirit to guide her instead of acting on her own will. When she gave up her own desires and allowed the Holy Spirit to lead her, He directed her to the center of God's will.

You may wonder: *How do I do that? How do I know that I'm living in the center of His will instead of acting on my own desires?* Jesus chose you and called you to do His will. Because you have chosen to deny yourself, take up your cross, and follow Him, He is now your Savior and Master. This week you will examine guidelines for doing God's will.

DAILY MASTER COMMUNICATION GUIDE

LUKE 2:41-52

What God said to me:

Just as I told you this morning. You take care of my business and I will take care of yours.

What I said to God:

Yes Lord, help me to stay on track and not allow myself to try to handle my business but If I seek you first. All my concerns are taken care of.

" 'This day I call heaven and earth as witnesses against you that I have set before you life and death, blessings and curses. Now choose life, so that you and your children may live and that you may love the Lord your God, listen to his voice, and hold fast to him. For the Lord is your life, and he will give you many years in the land he swore to give to your fathers, Abraham, Isaac and Jacob' " (Deut. 30:19-20).

"I know that nothing good lives in me, that is, in my sinful nature. For I have the desire to do what is good, but I cannot carry it out" (Rom. 7:18).

"Be very careful, then, how you live—not as unwise but as wise, making the most of every opportunity, because the days are evil. Therefore do not be foolish, but understand what the Lord's will is" (Eph. 5:15-17).

When you have completed this week's study, you should be able to—

- distinguish between God's will and your will;
- state God's purpose in your doing His will;
- explain the process and the provision by which God accomplishes His will;
- apply to your life the teachings about God's will.

YOU CAN CHOOSE

The Bible teaches that God has given you the capacity to purpose and to choose. This capacity is called your will. The Bible refers to will as a desire, intent, or purpose to do something.

Read the verses in the margin, which refer to a person's will. Indicate whether you agree with each statement:

1. A person's will can be used for good or evil. ❑ Yes ❑ No
2. God is always in control of a person's will. ❑ Yes ❑ No
3. A person can always do what he or she wills to do. ❑ Yes ❑ No

You may think that you are in control of your will, but your sinful nature may prevent your doing good. God wants you to do right, but He leaves that ultimate choice to you. In making your choice, you can choose good or evil. God wants you to choose His way, and His heart breaks when you choose ways that turn you away from Him. This week's Scripture-memory verse reminds you: "It is God who works in you to will and to act according to his good purpose" (Phil. 2:13). The correct answers are 1. yes, 2. no, 3. no.

God does not omit anyone in accomplishing His will. Every person is included in the scope of God's will. Second Peter 3:9 says, "The Lord is not slow in keeping his promise, as some understand slowness. He is patient with you, not wanting anyone to perish, but everyone to come to repentance." When a person becomes a Christian, the Holy Spirit begins revealing to that person God's will for his or her life. If you have life in the Spirit, you will experience this type of activity in your life.

Describe ways the Holy Spirit began revealing God's will in your life after you became a Christian.

____

____

Your answer may be similar to one of these statements: After I became a Christian, the Lord revealed that He wanted me to stop using profane language. He showed me that He wanted me to start attending church regularly. He pointed out that He wanted me to enter a church-related vocation.

The first four Scriptures in the margin mention God's will. Read them and mark the statements *T* (true) or *F* (false).

____ 1. Jesus claimed a special relationship with those who follow God's will.
____ 2. Jesus said that His purpose was to do God's will.
____ 3. Finding God's will is impossible.
____ 4. You can discover God's will.

Jesus said that those who do His will have a special relationship with Him. For Jesus, doing God's will was like food—a constant part of His obedient life and purpose. You can find God's will when you are willing to be transformed and to have a renewed mind. All of the statements are true except 3.

CHARACTERISTICS OF GOD'S WILL

God's will and the human will are vastly different. They differ in capacity and purpose. Your capacity to carry out your own will is limited. Even good purposes can be ill motivated and corrupted. For example, you could desire to win persons to the Lord so that others think you are a great Christian. You could also waver in your desire to reach persons for Christ. When the task becomes difficult, you could decide that it is not worth the effort.

Unlike your frail, human capacity, however, God's capacity to carry out His will is unlimited. His purpose is always holy, upright, and constant. He does not change His mind on a whim or when the way is difficult. He always wants His will to be done, and He sends His Holy Spirit to help accomplish it.

This week's Scripture-memory verse describes the way God works in you to help you find His will. To begin your memory work, read aloud Philippians 2:13 from one to three times. Check this box when you have done so: ❑

FULFILLING GOD'S PURPOSE

When you think about finding God's will for your life, you may wonder where to begin. You may feel that you cannot think God's thoughts or learn what He has in store for you. God wants to teach you how He reveals His will and how you can do His will. Doing God's will begins when you have a vision of God and His purpose for your life and are open to letting the Holy Spirit teach you.

Read Ephesians 1:5-6,12-14 in the margin. Check what these verses emphasize as God's primary purpose for your life.

❑ 1. To make me happy
❑ 2. To win the lost
❑ 3. To bring glory to God

" 'Whoever does the will of my Father in heaven is my brother and sister and mother' " (Matt. 12:50).

" 'My food,' said Jesus, 'is to do the will of him who sent me and to finish his work' " (John 4:34).

"Do not conform any longer to the pattern of this world, but be transformed by the renewing of your mind. Then you will be able to test and approve what God's will is—his good, pleasing and perfect will" (Rom. 12:2).

"For this reason, since the day we heard about you, we have not stopped praying for you and asking God to fill you with the knowledge of his will through all spiritual wisdom and understanding" (Col. 1:9).

"He predestined us to be adopted as his sons through Jesus Christ, in accordance with his pleasure and will—to the praise of his glorious grace, which he has freely given us in the One he loves.

"In order that we, who were the first to hope in Christ, might be for the praise of his glory. And you also were included in Christ when you heard the word of truth, the gospel of your salvation. Having believed, you were marked in him with a seal, the promised Holy Spirit, who is a deposit guaranteeing our inheritance until the redemption of those who are God's possession—to the praise of his glory" (Eph. 1:5-6,12-14).

Your purpose for living is to bring glory to God so that His name will be praised. The correct answer is 3.

Jesus' life depicts someone whose purpose for living was to bring glory to God so that His name would be praised. Jesus lived to do God's will. The Scriptures in the margin express how Jesus felt about doing God's will.

" 'Father, if you are willing, take this cup from me; yet not my will, but yours be done' " (Luke 22:42).

" 'By myself I can do nothing; I judge only as I hear, and my judgment is just, for I seek not to please myself but him who sent me' " (John 5:30).

" 'I have come down from heaven not to do my will but to do the will of him who sent me' " (John 6:38).

" 'I have brought you glory on earth by completing the work you gave me to do' " (John 17:4).

Read the Scriptures in the margin. Then match each Scripture reference with its summary statement.

C 1. Luke 22:42 **a. Jesus glorified God while He was on earth.**
B 2. John 5:30 **b. Jesus did not seek His own will.**
D 3. John 6:38 **c. Jesus prayed for God's will, not His, to be done.**
A 4. John 17:4 **d. Jesus came from heaven to do God's will.**

Jesus sought God's will while He was on earth and did not seek to do His own will. Would a person deliberately wish humiliation, anguish, and death for himself? If Jesus could have had His way, would He have chosen for friends and family to reject Him and for crowds to mock and scorn Him? Jesus experienced these things because they were part of His Father's perfect will, not because He wanted them. The correct answers are 1. c, 2. b, 3. d, 4. a.

Jesus' commitment to God's purpose made His ministry on this earth effective. Your development in every part of your Christian life and ministry depends on your commitment to God's purpose. Can you let Jesus be your example and guide in doing God's will?

Can you honestly state that the purpose of your life is to glorify God? ☑ Yes ☐ No If you could not answer yes, what takes priority over glorifying God? ____________________

What changes would you need to make for your life purpose to be glorifying God?

____

You can find God's will by regularly feeding on His Word and by spending time with Him in prayer. In *MasterLife 1: The Disciple's Cross* you learned the disciplines of living in the Word and praying in faith. I hope that having a daily quiet time, which incorporates these two disciplines, is a regular part of your life now. Each day during this study you will be asked to have a quiet time.

Read Luke 2:41-52, an early example of Jesus' doing His Father's will, during your quiet time today. Then complete the Daily Master Communication Guide on page 9.

DAY 2

About Your Personality

Do you ever wonder why you have thoughts, feelings, and behaviors that do not honor Christ?

As you studied about doing God's will in day 1, did you wonder why you often try to carry out your own will instead of first seeking God's will? Do you ever wonder why you have thoughts, feelings, and behaviors that do not honor Christ? Today you will begin learning the Disciple's Personality, a simple illustration that is a major part of our study of life in the Spirit. The drawing will illustrate biblical teachings about your personality. It will show you how to make Christ the Master of your life and how to master life as you strive to do God's will instead of your own.

LEARNING THE DISCIPLE'S PERSONALITY

God created you as a physical and spiritual being. The physical part came from the earth. The spiritual part originated in God's Spirit. The illustration you will draw over the next few days will help you understand how you are made.

The first part of the Disciple's Personality is called "A Unified Personality." Read that section on page 133. Begin by drawing a circle below, leaving openings at the top and the bottom of the circle. Write *God* above the circle. Refer to the Disciple's Personality presentation (pp. 133–39) if you need help.

The Bible describes you as a unity, a whole. That is why you drew one circle to represent your total personality. When you learned the Disciple's Cross, you drew a circle representing your life, with Christ at the center. In the Disciple's Personality presentation the circle also represents you. As you develop your understanding of your personality and behavior, you will add to your drawing. When you understand each element of your personality and how it functions, you will discover how to integrate your personality under the lordship of Christ. The Disciple's Personality also encourages you to continue practicing the six disciplines you learned in *MasterLife 1: The Disciple's Cross.* By the end of this study you will be able to draw the complete Disciple's Personality.

GROWING IN CHRISTLIKENESS

The Bible emphasizes building Christlike character, which is a part of the following definition of *discipleship.*

> Discipleship is developing a personal, lifelong, obedient relationship with Jesus Christ in which **He transforms your character into Christlikeness; changes your values into Kingdom values;** and involves you in His mission in the home, the church, and the world.

As you complete this study, you will work on aspects of your character that Christ desires to mold into His likeness. When you read this definition, you may have asked yourself: *What exactly is Christlikeness? How will I know whether my character is Christlike?*

"We know that in all things God works for the good of those who love him, who have been called according to his purpose. For those God foreknew he also predestined to be conformed to the likeness of his Son, that he might be the firstborn among many brothers" (Rom. 8:28-29).

Read the verses in the margin. What is God's will for you?

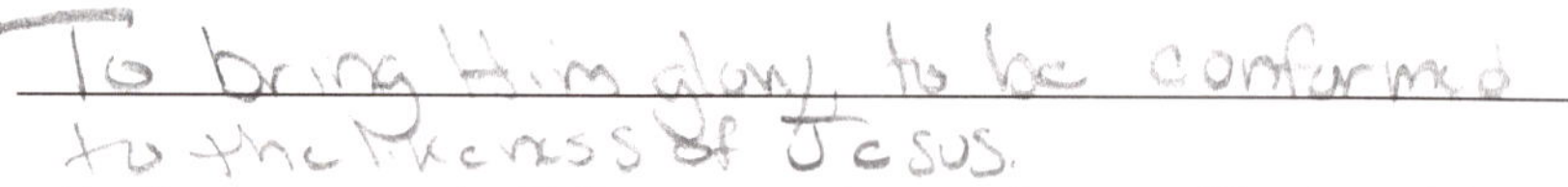

God's purpose and will for you are that you become like Jesus. Transforming your character into Christlikeness means that the Holy Spirit helps you increasingly become like Christ in every character trait.

In day 1 you read that Jesus did God's will. He came from heaven to do God's will. Doing God's will was a constant part of Jesus' obedient life and purpose. He glorified God while He was on earth. He prayed for God's will, not His own, to be done.

Do you desire to do what Jesus did? Check the statements that apply to you.

- ❑ **I want to be like Jesus and to do God's will, but I'm afraid that it may require me to give up something.**
- ❑ **I want to be like Jesus and to do God's will, but I'm afraid that I don't have the ability to do as He directs me.**
- ❑ **Being like Jesus is impossible for me. I can never do God's will if this is required of me.**
- ❑ **Yes, I want to do God's will, as Jesus did. Lord, please show me how.**

In this study you will learn more about how to be like Jesus, how increasingly to develop Christlike character, and how developing His character traits helps you do His will.

Say aloud this week's Scripture-memory verse, Philippians 2:13. Write what God says to you through this verse about doing God's will and about building Christlike character.

That He works in me to get this accomplished if I allow it

You may have answered something like this: I need to allow the Holy Spirit to work in me to remove harmful character traits and build new ones that honor Christ.

How are you doing in your practice of having a daily quiet time? Your goal is to have quiet times 21 straight days to establish it as part of your daily life. I hope that having a quiet time is a meaningful experience for you.

Read John 5:16-30 during your quiet time today. See what God reveals to you through this passage about another time Jesus mentioned pleasing the Father. Then complete the Daily Master Communication Guide in the margin.

DAILY MASTER COMMUNICATION GUIDE

JOHN 5:16-30

What God said to me:

As long as you have received instruction from me Do it even as those come against you or persecute you allow Me only to validate + vindicate who you are Not man

What I said to God:

Yes Lord let your will be done in my life, transform me more into your image

DAY 3

Committing Your Personality

Doing God's will depends on committing your whole personality to God. Even when you commit yourself to God, you soon discover that doing His will is not easy. Many factors influence you.

Schoolteacher Connie Baldwin described this type of struggle when she and her husband, Mark, a church-staff member, were searching to know God's will several years ago. "Mark felt that God was leading him to another church, but he didn't know where," Connie said. "He received a few offers but turned them down, saying he didn't feel that these offers were part of God's will. Unfortunately, I didn't have as much faith. I felt that Mark was crazy for turning down those churches."

The Holy Spirit then led Connie to Ephesians 3:20-21, which says that God is able to do immeasurably more than all we ask or imagine. "I realized that I was wrong to limit God's will and to mistrust my husband's faith. Then God called us to the church where we now serve. I never expected God's call to be to a church so loving, so God-centered, so caring—yet God knew all along!" Connie said that her lack of faith could have caused the couple to miss truly knowing and doing God's will and the Holy Spirit's leading.

"It is God who works in you to will and to act according to his good purpose" (Phil. 2:13).

"Do not conform any longer to the pattern of this world, but be transformed by the renewing of your mind. Then you will be able to test and approve what God's will is—his good, pleasing and perfect will" (Rom. 12:2).

"Offer your bodies as living sacrifices, holy and pleasing to God—this is your spiritual act of worship" (Rom. 12:1).

"The acts of the sinful nature are obvious: sexual immorality, impurity and debauchery; idolatry and witchcraft; hatred, discord, jealousy, fits of rage, selfish ambition, dissensions, factions and envy; drunkenness, orgies, and the like. I warn you, as I did before, that those who live like this will not inherit the kingdom of God. But the fruit of the Spirit is love, joy, peace, patience, kindness, goodness, faithfulness, gentleness and self-control. Against such things there is no law. Those who belong to Christ Jesus have crucified the sinful nature with its passions and desires" (Gal. 5:19-24).

"I have been crucified with Christ and I no longer live, but Christ lives in me. The life I lived in the body, I live by faith in the Son of God, who loved me and gave himself for me" (Gal. 2:20).

GOD PROVIDES THE WAY

Read 1 John 2:15-17 below.

> *"Do not love the world or anything in the world. If anyone loves the world, the love of the Father is not in him. For everything in the world—the cravings of sinful man, the lust of his eyes and the boasting of what he has and does—comes not from the Father but from the world. The world and its desires pass away, but the man who does the will of God lives forever" (1 John 2:15-17).*

Check the factor(s) that most hinder you from doing God's will.
❑ sinful nature ❑ environment ❑ heredity

Although you may have checked more than one answer, the verses from 1 John clearly indicate that your sinful nature keeps you from doing God's will. Other factors may predispose you to it. You may live in an environment in which sin is rampant. You may come from a family that did not honor Christ. But you have a choice about whether to do God's will. Your sinful nature is the primary culprit that causes you to refuse to listen to the Holy Spirit and decline to do God's will.

How do you commit your whole personality to God? Does that mean losing your identity? Does that mean becoming passive and simply letting life roll over you? Does that mean never again struggling with what God wants you to do? Even Jesus struggled when He was tempted. But even though you struggle, God provides a way to accomplish His will in you when you commit your entire personality to Him.

Read the Scriptures in the margin. Describe how God enables you to commit each part of your personality to His will. The first reference is this week's Scripture-memory verse. See if you can recite it from memory.

Will (Phil. 2:13): ____________________

Mind (Rom. 12:2): ____________________

Body (Rom. 12:1): ____________________

Emotions (Gal. 5:19-24): ____________________

Life (Gal. 2:20): ____________________

Here are some ways you could have answered: *Will:* God works in you to provide the will and the ability to do His good pleasure. *Mind*: God renews your mind so that you can prove that His will is good, pleasing, and complete. *Body:* God tells you to present your body as a living sacrifice to Him as your reasonable service; Jesus encourages you to pray because your body is weak (see Matt. 26:41). *Emotions:* The Holy Spirit produces the fruit of the Spirit in you to replace evil emotions and actions. *Life:* Christ lives in you when you are crucified with Him, and He provides the power to do His will.

Here is a summary of what you have learned about God's will:

The process of doing God's will is accomplished through—
- a vision of God's purpose for your life;
- a commitment of your whole personality to God;
- actions based on God's provision for doing His will.

LEARNING THE DISCIPLE'S PERSONALITY

The Bible depicts you as a body and a soul. Read the sections "Body" and "Soul" (pp. 133–34) in the Disciple's Personality presentation.

Draw a circle with *God* above it and *body* beneath it. Write the five senses—*sight, sound, smell, taste,* and *touch*—on each side of the circle. Now write *soul* on the inner top rim of the circle and *mind, will,* and *emotions* in the exact center of the circle. Refer to the Disciple's Personality presentation (pp. 133–39) if you need help. By the end of this study you will be able to draw the complete Disciple's Personality and to explain it in your own words.

Daily Master Communication Guide

Exodus 4:1-17

What God said to me:

What I said to God:

What happens when you shift from the image of self to the image of Christ? What happens when you set aside the inclinations of the natural person and increasingly become more Christlike? In day 2 you learned that God expects you to be like Jesus, becoming more Christlike day by day. Today you will learn more about what that means.

IN THE CARPENTER'S SHOP

When you think about setting aside old traits and becoming more Chistlike, you can picture tearing down an old house and building a new one. What will you tear down and replace to become more Christlike? Ask the Holy Spirit to show you as you read Galatians 5:16-25 in the margin.

"Live by the Spirit, and you will not gratify the desires of the sinful nature. For the sinful nature desires what is contrary to the Spirit, and the Spirit what is contrary to the sinful nature. They are in conflict with each other, so that you do not do what you want. But if you are led by the Spirit, you are not under law.

"The acts of the sinful nature are obvious: sexual immorality, impurity and debauchery; idolatry and witchcraft; hatred, discord, jealousy, fits of rage, selfish ambition, dissensions, factions and envy; drunkenness, orgies, and the like. I warn you, as I did before, that those who live like this will not inherit the kingdom of God. But the fruit of the Spirit is love, joy, peace, patience, kindness, goodness, faithfulness, gentleness and self-control. Against such things there is no law. Those who belong to Christ Jesus have crucified the sinful nature with its passions and desires. Since we live by the Spirit, let us keep in step with the Spirit" (Gal. 5:16-25).

Galatians 5:16-25 is one of three similar Bible passages that illustrate what it means to leave the old life behind, or tear it down, and to take up, or build, the new life. You will study the other two passages in days 4 and 5 this week.

Below are statements from the passage you just read from Galatians 5. Write *O* beside the statements that apply to the old person in Christ and *N* beside those that describe a new person in Christ.

_____ 1. "Keep in step with the Spirit."
_____ 2. "Gratify the desires of the sinful nature."
_____ 3. "[Desire] what is contrary to the Spirit."
_____ 4. "[Crucify] the sinful nature."
_____ 5. "Live by the Spirit."
_____ 6. "[Be] led by the Spirit."
_____ 7. "[Have] the fruit of the Spirit."

As you know Christ more intimately, your life will change. You want to do God's will, to be like Christ, and to have Christ's character. The answers are 1. N, 2. O, 3. O, 4. N, 5. N, 6. N, 7. N.

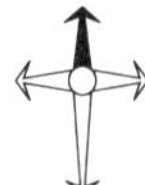

Stop and pray for the salvation of the non-Christian friends group members mentioned during group session 1.

In this study you are using your Daily Master Communication Guide to record what God says to you and what you say to God. You may want to begin keeping a journal so that you will have more room to write. I suggest that you use *Day by Day in God's Kingdom: A Discipleship Journal.* This journal not only suggests Scriptures and memory verses but also provides room for you to record what you experience in your quiet time.[1]

Read Exodus 4:1-17 during your quiet time today. See how God speaks to you through this passage about Moses' struggle with doing God's will. Then complete the Daily Master Communication Guide on page 17.

DAY 4

Supplying Your Need

When you think about doing God's will, you may feel helpless. You may believe that you need to be a scholar with vast theological knowledge. You may feel that only a pastor, an evangelist, or someone who studies the Bible and prays around the clock can be enough in tune with God to detect His will under the Holy Spirit's leading.

But the Scriptures say that God provides you exactly what you need to achieve His will. Both Philippians 4:19 and Romans 8:28, in the margin, illustrate how well He equips you to know His will.

Read the verses in the margin. Describe what God has promised to do.

"My God will meet all your needs according to his glorious riches in Christ Jesus" (Phil. 4:19).

"We know that in all things God works for the good of those who love him, who have been called according to his purpose" (Rom. 8:28).

Philippians 4:19: ______________________________

____

Romans 8:28: ______________________________

____

These passages provide marvelous reassurance that extraordinary knowledge or intellect is not required to know God's will. He will supply your needs and will work all things together for good.

Describe a time when God supplied your needs so that you could know His will.

____

You might read these verses and think, *If all of my needs are supplied, I can make it without God.* But doing God's will on your own is impossible. Only God has the capacity to do exactly what He intends. Doing God's will involves a process in which God uses the provisions He has given you to accomplish His work. The two verses in the margin describe this process.

"Being confident of this, that he who began a good work in you will carry it on to completion until the day of Christ Jesus" (Phil. 1:6).

"The one who calls you is faithful and he will do it" (1 Thess. 5:24).

In the margin write from memory this week's Scripture-memory verse, Philippians 2:13. Describe in your own words how God accomplishes His will in you.

____

You may have answered something like this: God works in me to will and to do what pleases Him. He also gives me the ability to do His will.

Reread Philippians 1:6 in the margin on page 19. What good work do you think Christ has begun in you?

____

How can you see that He is being faithful to complete this good work in you?

____

Perhaps you believe that one of the good works Christ has begun in you is a new willingness to witness to the world. Perhaps you have begun to see new opportunities to witness that you never thought about before. Perhaps you have begun to build relationships with persons that will provide entry points for you to witness. Christ promises that He will be faithful to complete work He has begun in you. He has given you the task of witnessing, and He will strengthen you for it.

Christ promises that He will be faithful to complete work He has begun in you.

Think of five persons who need you to witness to them. Write their names on your Prayer-Covenant List. (You learned in *MasterLife 1: The Disciple's Cross* how to keep such a list. Use the form on p. 143 to start a list if you are not already keeping one.) If you cannot think of five unsaved persons, begin making friends with others so that you can witness to them in the future.

You may desire to do God's will, but internal conflicts and barriers may arise. That is why it is important to continue learning to integrate your personality under the lordship of Christ. As you study the Disciple's Personality today, you will learn how the Bible pictures you as spirit and will understand how His will can truly be done in you as you live in the Holy Spirit.

LEARNING THE DISCIPLE'S PERSONALITY

Read the section "Spirit" (p. 134) in the Disciple's Personality presentation. Read the two verses in the margin to learn how the Bible pictures you as spirit.

"Who among men knows the thoughts of a man except the man's spirit within him? In the same way no one knows the thoughts of God except the Spirit of God" (1 Cor. 2:11).

"The Spirit himself testifies with our spirit that we are God's children" (Rom. 8:16).

On the next page draw a circle, leaving openings at the top and bottom. Write *God* above it and *body* beneath it. Write the five senses—*sight, sound, smell, taste,* and *touch*—on each side of the circle. Write *soul* inside the top rim of the circle and *mind, will,* and *emotions* in the exact center. Write *spirit* vertically down the center of the circle, stopping at the word *will.* Refer to

the Disciple's Personality presentation (pp. 133–39) if you need help. By the end of this study you will be able to draw the complete Disciple's Personality and to explain it in your own words.

IN THE CARPENTER'S SHOP

As you become more like Christ, with the Holy Spirit's help you will continue to put aside, or tear down, traits of the old person and to substitute traits of the new person. The verses from Colossians 3, in the margin, illustrate what leaving the old life behind and taking up the new one mean.

Read in the margin the passage from Colossians 3. Underline statements that describe the tendencies of the old life before Christ. Circle statements describing the tendencies of the new life after Christ.

I hope that this exercise continued to emphasize what must happen for you to become like Christ. For the old life, you may have underlined such phrases as "rid yourselves of all such things," "Put to death, therefore, whatever belongs to your earthly nature," and "you have taken off your old self with its practices." For the new life, you may have circled "set your hearts on things above," "Set your minds on things above," "clothe yourselves with compassion, kindness, humility, gentleness and patience," and "over all these virtues put on love, which binds them all together in perfect unity."

"Since, then, you have been raised with Christ, set your hearts on things above, where Christ is seated at the right hand of God. Set your minds on things above, not on earthly things. For you died, and your life is now hidden with Christ in God. When Christ, who is your life, appears, then you also will appear with him in glory.

"Put to death, therefore, whatever belongs to your earthly nature: sexual immorality, impurity, lust, evil desires and greed, which is idolatry. Because of these, the wrath of God is coming. You used to walk in these ways, in the life you once lived. But now you must rid yourselves of all such things as these: anger, rage, malice, slander, and filthy language from your lips. Do not lie to each other, since you have taken off your old self with its practices and have put on the new self, which is being renewed in knowledge in the image of its Creator. Here there is no Greek or Jew, circumcised or uncircumcised, barbarian, Scythian, slave or free, but Christ is all, and is in all.

"Therefore, as God's chosen people, holy and dearly loved, clothe yourselves with compassion, kindness, humility, gentleness and patience. Bear with each other and forgive whatever grievances you may have against one another. Forgive as the Lord forgave you. And over all these virtues put on love, which binds them all together in perfect unity" (Col. 3:1-14).

Daily Master Communication Guide

Job 42

What God said to me:

____

____

____

____

____

____

____

____

What I said to God:

____

____

____

____

____

____

____

____

____

Read Job 42 during your quiet time today, describing the way God supplied the needs of someone who did His will. Then complete the Daily Master Communication Guide in the margin.

Sometimes people ask me: "Do I need to be alone when I have my quiet time? Can I have a quiet time with my spouse or family?" Certainly, having couple or family devotions and praying and studying the Bible with a friend are excellent ways to spend time with the Master. (You will learn more about conversational prayer during this study.) But these cannot take the place of individual time you spend with Christ. Kay Moore, who wrote this book with me, prays and reads the Bible with her husband when they awake every morning. During this time they place before God their family's needs and seek His direction for their lives that day. Later in the day, before she begins working at her desk, Kay has her own private devotional time with God. Her husband, Louis, has his personal quiet time during his lunch hour after eating at his desk.

Make sure that your day includes a personal quiet time.

Ask God to help you continue to find the right time and setting each day to devote to a quiet time with Him.

DAY 5

Shutting the Door of the Flesh

You may think that you are the only person who struggles with knowing God's will. Perhaps you think that people in Bible times whom God used to accomplish His purposes automatically knew exactly what God wanted them to do and never considered their own preferences. You may think that their lives were easy because they chose God's way.

Your daily Bible passages this week have focused on Bible figures and their struggles to do God's will. In today's study you will examine three more. Read about Moses, Jesus, and Paul in the Scriptures in the margin on the next page.

Moses, Jesus, and Paul willingly suffered in order to follow God's will. Each displayed these three components of doing God's will:

Doing God's will is accomplished through—
- ❑ a vision of God's purpose for your life;
- ❑ a commitment of your entire personality to God;
- ❑ actions based on God's provision for doing His will.

In the previous box check the component you believe is the most difficult for you in your effort to do God's will.

CONFORMED TO HIS LIKENESS

Read Romans 8:29: "Those God foreknew he also predestined to be conformed to the likeness of his Son, that he might be the firstborn among many brothers." This verse says that if God's will is accomplished in your life, you will be conformed to the likeness of Christ, God's Son. You will act like Him, will think like Him, and will have the kind of relationships with God and others that Christ did. You will have Him at the center of your life, and you will yield to the Holy Spirit's leading in your life.

Say aloud this week's Scripture-memory verse, Philippians 2:13, to someone in your family or to a close friend. Tell that person how this verse has made you more aware of doing God's will.

Apply this verse to your life by writing your personal response to each of the following statements.

The vision I have of God's purpose for my life is—

____.

If I said, "I commit my whole personality to God," that would mean that I—

____.

Because I know that God will provide for me when I do His will, I will take the following action(s):

____

____

What hinders you from keeping these commitments? A look at the Natural Person, another part of the Disciple's Personality, provides an answer.

LEARNING THE DISCIPLE'S PERSONALITY

Today you will begin learning the Natural Person part of the Disciple's Personality. Read the section "The Flesh" (p. 134) in the Disciple's Personality presentation.

The Bible uses the word *flesh* in two ways.

"By faith Moses, when he had grown up, refused to be known as the son of Pharaoh's daughter. He chose to be mistreated along with the people of God rather than to enjoy the pleasures of sin for a short time. He regarded disgrace for the sake of Christ as of greater value than the treasures of Egypt, because he was looking ahead to his reward. By faith he left Egypt, not fearing the king's anger; he persevered because he saw him who is invisible" (Heb. 11:24-27).

"[Jesus] withdrew about a stone's throw beyond them, knelt down and prayed, 'Father, if you are willing, take this cup from me; yet not my will, but yours be done' " (Luke 22: 41-42).

"If anyone else thinks he has reasons to put confidence in the flesh, I [Paul] have more: circumcised on the eighth day, of the people of Israel, of the tribe of Benjamin, a Hebrew of Hebrews; in regard to the law, a Pharisee; as for zeal, persecuting the church; as for legalistic righteousness, faultless.

"But whatever was to my profit I now consider loss for the sake of Christ. What is more, I consider everything a loss compared to the surpassing greatness of Christ Jesus my Lord, for whose sake I have lost all things. I consider them rubbish, that I may gain Christ" (Phil. 3:4-8).

"Do not let sin reign in your mortal body so that you obey its evil desires" (Rom. 6:12).

"Live by the Spirit, and you will not gratify the desires of the sinful nature. For the sinful nature desires what is contrary to the Spirit, and the Spirit what is contrary to the sinful nature. They are in conflict with each other, so that you do not do what you want. But if you are led by the Spirit, you are not under law" (Gal. 5:16-18).

Read the two verses in the margin and describe the two ways these verses refer to flesh.

Romans 6:12: ______________________________

Galatians 5:16-18: ______________________________

The general meaning of *flesh* is body, referring to the physical body (see Rom. 6:12). The other meaning is symbolic, referring to the lower nature (see Gal. 5:16-18). The *King James Version* uses *flesh* to mean *sinful nature.* It refers to the human capacity to sin and to follow Satan instead of God.

Draw the portions of the Disciple's Personality you learned this week. Close the door of the spirit by completing the circle at the top. Leave the door of the flesh open at the bottom of the circle. Now draw an *I* in the center of the circle that surrounds the words *spirit* and *will.* Write *flesh* vertically under *will.* Draw a line through *spirit.* Write *Satan* outside the circle beneath *body.* Then write *1 Corinthians 2:14* above *God* and label your drawing *The Natural Person.* Refer to the Disciple's Personality presentation (pp. 133–39) if you need help. By the end of this study you will be able to draw the entire Disciple's Personality and to explain it in your own words.

Now read the section "The Condition of the Natural Person Today" (p. 135) in the Disciple's Personality presentation. These teachings help you understand why even a natural person's best intentions sometimes fail when he or she wants to do right but cannot seem to. During the coming weeks, learning the Disciple's Personality will help you compare the way you live to God's plan for you.

How have you kept the door of the flesh open in your life? On a separate sheet of paper write the things you do that displease God. Confess your sins to God. Read 1 John 1:9: "If we confess our sins, he is faithful and just and will forgive us our sins and purify us from all unrighteousness." Accept that God has forgiven you. Tear up or burn the list to signify that your sins are forgiven.

Pray that as God works through the Holy Spirit, He will help you keep the commitments you wrote on page 23 and will shut the door of the flesh, which would prevent your carrying them out.

IN THE CARPENTER'S SHOP

Read in the margin the verses from Ephesians to continue learning how to build Christlike character. In the left column write statements that refer to actions of the old person. In the right column write statements that describe what a new person does after coming to know Christ.

Old Person	New Person
______________________	______________________
______________________	______________________
______________________	______________________

For actions of the old person, you may have listed "no longer live as the Gentiles do," "put off your old self," or "do not grieve the Holy Spirit." For steps that the new person would take, you may have listed "be made new in the attitude of your minds; and to put on the new self," "be like God in true righteousness and holiness," or "live a life of love." As you learn to live like Jesus, you will learn that the ways of the world present a stark contrast to the Christian lifestyle.

Putting on the new person may involve new attitudes toward your family members.

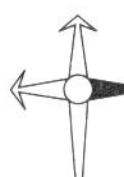

Spend time with a member of your family, maybe one with whom you have not talked in a long time. Write or call the person if he or she does not live in your locale.

"I tell you this, and insist on it in the Lord, that you must no longer live as the Gentiles do, in the futility of their thinking. They are darkened in their understanding and separated from the life of God because of the ignorance that is in them due to the hardening of their hearts. Having lost all sensitivity, they have given themselves over to sensuality so as to indulge in every kind of impurity, with a continual lust for more.

"You, however, did not come to know Christ that way. Surely you heard of him and were taught in him in accordance with the truth that is in Jesus. You were taught, with regard to your former way of life, to put off your old self, which is being corrupted by its deceitful desires; to be made new in the attitude of your minds; and to put on the new self, created to be like God in true righteousness and holiness.

"And do not grieve the Holy Spirit of God, with whom you were sealed for the day of redemption. Get rid of all bitterness, rage and anger, brawling and slander, along with every form of malice. Be kind and compassionate to one another, forgiving each other, just as in Christ God forgave you.

"Be imitators of God, therefore, as dearly loved children and live a life of love, just as Christ loved us and gave himself up for us as a fragrant offering and sacrifice to God" (Eph. 4:17-24,30—5:2).

Daily Master Communication Guide

Genesis 3:1-7

What God said to me:

What I said to God:

Read Genesis 3:1-7, about something that introduced problems into God's creation, during your quiet time today. Then complete the Daily Master Communication Guide in the margin.

HAS THIS WEEK MADE A DIFFERENCE?

Review "My Walk with the Master This Week" at the beginning of this week's material. Mark the activities you have finished by drawing vertical lines in the diamonds beside them. Finish any incomplete activities. Think about what you will say during your group session about your work on these activities.

To assess your progress this week, check the appropriate boxes.

- ❑ **I understand the roles played by body, soul, and spirit in forming my total personality.**
- ❑ **I understand the role the flesh plays in my personality to undermine my good intentions.**
- ❑ **Instead of seeking what I want, I strive to do God's will and to have Christ's character.**
- ❑ **Seeking God's will in decisions is a major part of my life in the Spirit.**
- ❑ **I truly desire to be like Jesus.**

From this week's study of "Do God's Will" you can see that keeping the door of the flesh closed and refusing to allow Satan to get a foothold in your life are challenges that require constant vigilance. Developing a daily quiet time and spending regular time with the Master allow the Holy Spirit to work in your life when it would be easier to keep the door of the flesh open.

[1]To order *Day by Day in God's Kingdom: A Discipleship Journal* (item 0-7673-2577-X): WRITE LifeWay Church Resources Customer Service, One LifeWay Plaza, Nashville, TN 37234-0113; FAX order to (615) 251-5933; PHONE 1-800-458-2772; E-MAIL *orderentry@lifeway.com*; order ONLINE at *www.lifeway.com*; or visit the LifeWay Christian Store serving you.

WEEK 2

Renew Your Mind

This Week's Goal

You will be able to renew your mind through the transforming power of the Word and Holy Spirit.

My Walk with the Master This Week

You will complete the following activities to develop the six biblical disciplines. When you have completed each activity, draw a vertical line in the diamond beside it.

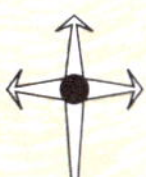

SPEND TIME WITH THE MASTER

◇ Have a quiet time each day, working toward the goal of having quiet times 21 consecutive days. Check the box beside each day you have a quiet time this week: ❑ Sunday ❑ Monday ❑ Tuesday ❑ Wednesday ❑ Thursday ❑ Friday ❑ Saturday

LIVE IN THE WORD

◇ Read your Bible every day. Write what God says to you and what you say to God.

◇ Memorize Romans 12:1-2.

◇ Review Philippians 2:13.

PRAY IN FAITH

◇ Pray with a friend, a family member, or your prayer partner.

◇ Teach someone "Principles of Conversational Prayer."

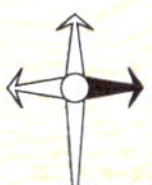

FELLOWSHIP WITH BELIEVERS

◇ Go out to dinner or plan a private time with your spouse or, if you are not married, a close friend. Talk about matters that are most important to you.

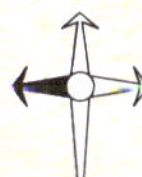

WITNESS TO THE WORLD

◇ Do something kind for a member of your immediate or extended family who does not know Christ.

MINISTER TO OTHERS

◇ Learn the Worldly Christian part of the Disciple's Personality.

This Week's Scripture-Memory Verses

"I urge you, brothers, in view of God's mercy, to offer your bodies as living sacrifices, holy and pleasing to God—this is your spiritual act of worship. Do not conform any longer to the pattern of this world, but be transformed by the renewing of your mind. Then you will be able to test and approve what God's will is—his good, pleasing and perfect will" (Rom. 12:1-2).

DAY 1

Making the Wrong Decisions

Your mind is much like a tape recorder or a video recorder. You record events and thoughts and continue to listen to them even when other options are open to you. These tapes from the past often lead you repeatedly to make the same wrong choices.

Paul described his situation in these words: "I do not understand what I do. For what I want to do I do not do, but what I hate I do. I know that nothing good lives in me, that is, in my sinful nature. For I have the desire to do what is good, but I cannot carry it out. For what I do is not the good I want to do; no, the evil I do not want to do—this I keep on doing. Now if I do what I do not want to do, it is no longer I who do it, but it is sin living in me that does it" (Rom. 7:15,18-20).

Like me, you sometimes feel as Paul did—that you are trapped with a sinful nature that does not want to do God's will. Even though you want to do what is right, your mind thinks about doing wrong. I believe that the devil plays tapes of wrong actions. As a result, you keep making wrong decisions.

" 'I will ask the Father, and he will give you another Counselor to be with you forever—the Spirit of truth. The world cannot accept him, because it neither sees him nor knows him. But you know him, for he lives with you and will be in you. I will not leave you as orphans; I will come to you. Before long, the world will not see me anymore, but you will see me. Because I live, you also will live. On that day you will realize that I am in my Father, and you are in me, and I am in you' " (John 14:16-20).

In Romans 7:25 Paul provided an answer to his dilemma: "Thanks be to God—through Jesus Christ our Lord!" He added in Romans 8:1-2, "There is now no condemnation for those who are in Christ Jesus, because through Christ Jesus the law of the Spirit of life set me free from the law of sin and death."

The Holy Spirit takes God's Word and the words spoken by Christ, makes them real, and applies them to your life.

Read John 14:16-20 in the margin and answer the following questions.

Why did Jesus say that He was sending the Holy Spirit?

As Cansel to be c with us forever.

____

How did Jesus say that the disciples would recognize the Holy Spirit?

As living within us

____

Jesus told the disciples that He was sending the Holy Spirit to provide the same kind of help, comfort, and teaching He had provided them while on earth. He said that they would know the Holy Spirit because He would live within them. The Holy Spirit does not merely walk alongside you but actually lives in your heart and life.

John 14:26, in the margin, also depicts the Holy Spirit as a counselor, or personal teacher. In this week's study you will discover how to let the Holy Spirit renew your mind. When you have completed this week's study, you should be able to—

- describe the difference between the natural mind and the renewed mind;
- explain what it means to have the mind of Christ in you;
- describe the process of renewal of the mind;
- identify at least three ways to be more spiritually minded.

" 'The Counselor, the Holy Spirit, whom the Father will send in my name, will teach you all things and will remind you of everything I have said to you' " (John 14:26).

FOLLOWING THE NATURAL MIND

When I talk about the natural mind, I am referring to the thinking process that is limited to human reason and resources (see 1 Cor. 2:14 in the margin). Human history shows that the natural mind becomes progressively self-destructive if left to its own desires.

"The man without the Spirit does not accept the things that come from the Spirit of God, for they are foolishness to him, and he cannot understand them, because they are spiritually discerned" (1 Cor. 2:14).

Read Ephesians 4:17-18 in the margin. What do these verses say about people who live according to their natural minds? Fill in the blanks.

Their thinking is ______________________.

They walk in the ______________________ of their understanding.

They are separated from God because of ______________.

They are ignorant because of their ______________.

"I tell you this, and insist on it in the Lord, that you must no longer live as the Gentiles do, in the futility of their thinking. They are darkened in their understanding and separated from the life of God because of the ignorance that is in them due to the hardening of their hearts" (Eph. 4:17-18).

People who follow their natural minds and live as these natural minds direct walk in darkness and have futile thinking. Ignorance, which results because their hearts are hardened, separates them from God. They live hopeless lives.

The natural mind inevitably becomes enslaved to other masters. Romans 1:28-31 says: "Since they did not think it worthwhile to retain the knowledge of God, he gave them over to a depraved mind, to do what ought not to be done. They have become filled with every kind of wickedness, evil, greed and depravity. They are full of envy, murder, strife, deceit and malice. They are gossips, slanderers, God-haters, insolent, arrogant and boastful; they invent ways of doing evil; they disobey their parents; they are senseless, faithless, heartless, ruthless." The natural mind in turn enslaves a personality by reducing it primarily to the world of the senses and evil.

To what masters are you enslaved? Meditate on the words in Romans 1:28-31 in the previous paragraph. Can you identify with some of these masters? If you can, underline the types of wrong-doing with which you struggle.

Read the Scriptures in the margin. Then draw a line between each word in the left column that describes the natural mind and the Scripture reference in the right column in which the word is found.

depraved	**2 Corinthians 4:4**
unspiritual	**Romans 1:28**
blinded	**1 Timothy 6:5**
corrupt	**Colossians 2:18**

"The god of this age has blinded the minds of unbelievers, so that they cannot see the light of the gospel of the glory of Christ, who is the image of God" (2 Cor. 4:4).

"Since they did not think it worthwhile to retain the knowledge of God, he gave them over to a depraved mind, to do what ought not to be done" (Rom. 1:28).

" … constant friction between men of corrupt mind, who have been robbed of the truth and who think that godliness is a means to financial gain" (1 Tim. 6:5).

"Do not let anyone who delights in false humility and the worship of angels disqualify you for the prize. Such a person goes into great detail about what he has seen, and his unspiritual mind puffs him up with idle notions" (Col. 2:18).

These Scriptures clearly teach what happens to a person whose mind is not focused as the Spirit directs. The words used to describe such an existence are horrifying. The correct answers are: *depraved*, Romans 1:28; *unspiritual*, Colossians 2:18; *blinded*, 2 Corinthians 4:4; *corrupt*, 1 Timothy 6:5.

THE RENEWED MIND

The Holy Spirit uses God's Word to renew a person's mind. The natural mind and the renewed mind have the same basic functions: thinking, judging, reasoning, and evaluating. The difference is who controls these processes.

Turn to page 27 and read this week's Scripture-memory verses, Romans 12:1-2. Begin to memorize them as you reflect on what they say about the renewed mind. Review page 112 in *MasterLife 1: The Disciple's Cross* if you need to to recall memorization methods.

The renewed mind is obedient to Christ. The natural mind thinks from a humanistic, sin-debased viewpoint. The renewed mind frees the personality by enlarging it to encompass the world of the Spirit in addition to the senses.

Write *N* beside the statements that describe the natural mind and *R* beside the ones that describe the renewed mind.

N **1. Becomes progressively self-destructive**
N **2. Is limited to purely human reason and resources**
R **3. Thinks from Christ's viewpoint as the Holy Spirit directs**
R **4. Frees the personality by including the Spirit**
N **5. Thinks from the viewpoint of the flesh**

The natural mind leads to a path of self-destruction. It does not rely on the mind of Christ but is limited to the resources of the human mind. The viewpoint of the flesh directs its thoughts. On the other hand, the renewed mind thinks from Christ's viewpoint as guided by the Holy Spirit. The correct answers are 1. N, 2. N, 3. R, 4. R, 5. N.

When the Holy Spirit rules your mind, you obey Christ. You think, *What would Christ have me do in this situation?* You try to understand what the Holy Spirit, who lives in you as your personal teacher, is leading you to do.

In contrast, fleshly, worldly thoughts rule the worldly, sinful mind.

Read Romans 8:1-14 in your Bible and mark the following statements *T* (true) or *F* (false).

F 1. The worldly mind concentrates on spiritual things.
T 2. To set your mind on things of the flesh brings death.
T 3. The worldly mind does not submit to the Holy Spirit's control.
F 4. A worldly mind sometimes pleases God.
F 5. No hope exists for changing a worldly mind.

The worldly mind is in the control of Satan, not of the Holy Spirit. Setting your mind on things of the flesh without turning to Christ brings death. Yet persons who set aside worldly ways and turn over their lives and thoughts to Christ can know forgiveness and joy. You can have a spiritual mind even if a worldly mind has ruled you in the past. The correct answers are 1. F, 2. T, 3. T, 4. F, 5. F.

Again read Romans 8:1-14, which contrasts the worldly mind and the spiritual mind, during your quiet time today. Then complete the Daily Master Communication Guide in the margin.

In week 1 you were asked to spend time with a family member. This week go out to dinner or plan a private time with your spouse or, if you are not married, a close friend. Talk about the things that are most important. Satan would like nothing better than to gain control of your relationships, especially your home. Spending time with your spouse or someone close to you can help keep you from a path of self-destruction in your personal life. I pray that the Holy Spirit will direct you to give this relationship more emphasis.

Daily Master Communication Guide

Romans 8:1-14

What God said to me:

This is why I have been urging you to be obedient. I have had enough of people straddling the fence ē Me.

What I said to God:

Yes God, thank You for loving me enough to correct me and reveal yourself to me.

DAY 2

Ruled by the Flesh

When you studied about the natural person in week 1, you probably realized that this person does not know Christ. He or she lives a natural, unregenerate life without Christ.

"As for you, you were dead in your transgressions and sins, in which you used to live when you followed the ways of this world and of the ruler of the kingdom of the air, the spirit who is now at work in those who are disobedient. All of us also lived among them at one time, gratifying the cravings of our sinful nature and following its desires and thoughts. Like the rest, we were by nature objects of wrath" (Eph. 2:1-3).

"Because of his great love for us, God, who is rich in mercy, made us alive with Christ even when we were dead in transgressions—it is by grace you have been saved. And God raised us up with Christ and seated us with him in the heavenly realms in Christ Jesus, in order that in the coming ages he might show the incomparable riches of his grace, expressed in his kindness to us in Christ Jesus. For it is by grace you have been saved, through faith—and this not from yourselves, it is the gift of God—not by works, so that no one can boast. For we are God's workmanship, created in Christ Jesus to do good works, which God prepared in advance for us to do" (Eph. 2:4-10).

Read Ephesians 2:1-3 in the margin and underline the phrases that describe your former way of life.

Now read Ephesians 2:4-10 in the margin and underline what God did for you.

Before you knew Christ, you were dead in your transgressions and sins. When you repented of your sins and your sinful way of life and asked Christ to be your Savior and Lord, God made you alive with Christ. By His grace He saved you and raised you up with Christ. You are now God's workmanship, created in Christ Jesus to do good works.

However, many persons who have received Christ and have the Holy Spirit living in their hearts still do not live as God intended. That is why Paul told the Ephesians in Ephesians 4:17-24 that they had not learned the ways of the world from Christ and that they should move away from that way of living.

A WORLDLY CHRISTIAN

If a Christian lives like the unbelieving world, this person is a worldly Christian. The *King James Version* calls this person *carnal,* which means *fleshly.* It refers to a person who is governed by human nature more than by the Spirit of God. Paul contrasts spiritual people—those who are under the control of the Holy Spirit—with those who are carnal—those who are under the control of the flesh. First Corinthians 3:1 describes worldly Christians: "Brothers, I could not address you as spiritual but as worldly—mere infants in Christ."

Second Peter 1:3 makes clear that God has provided you His power: "His divine power has given us everything we need for life and godliness through our knowledge of him who called us by his own glory and goodness." He has given you the rich promise of eternal life. He has given you the resources you need for life and righteous living. However, a few verses later, in 2 Peter 1:5, you are told to add certain things to your faith that God has provided for you.

In 2 Peter 1:5-9, in the margin on the next page, underline the things you are told to add to your faith.

You likely underlined that you are to add to your faith goodness, knowledge, self-control, perseverance, godliness, brotherly kindness, and love. If you continue to manifest the traits of a worldly Christian—

- you are ineffective and unproductive. A worldly Christian is sluggish and does not grow in his or her faith. A worldly Christian does not have a productive life for Christ.
- you are nearsighted and blind. This person is blind to the Holy Spirit's truth and listens to Satan's lies.
- you have forgotten that you have been cleansed. This person has forgotten his cleansing from sin and does not appreciate God and Christ for his or her forgiveness.

"For this very reason, make every effort to add to your faith goodness; and to goodness, knowledge; and to knowledge, self-control; and to self-control, perseverance; and to perseverance, godliness; and to godliness, brotherly kindness; and to brotherly kindness, love. For if you possess these qualities in increasing measure, they will keep you from being ineffective and unproductive in your knowledge of our Lord Jesus Christ. But if anyone does not have them, he is nearsighted and blind, and has forgotten that he has been cleansed from his past sins" (2 Pet. 1:5-9).

Reread the results if persons do not grow and add to their faith. Check any results you see in your life.

MASTERING THE MIND

God never intends for a Christian to be worldly. Yet some Christians are. Probably because they have not been guided in how to grow, they are still guided more by fleshly desires than by spiritual desires. Christ secures your salvation, but you are still responsible for how you live. You are responsible for using His resources and for following Him.

The Holy Spirit wants to be to your mind what a rudder is to a ship. A rudder keeps the ship on course so that it arrives at its destination. In 2 Corinthians 10:3-5, in the margin, Paul described a two-step plan for mastering the human mind. Paul described an offensive-defensive game plan that worked for his life, as it will for yours. In the defensive game plan you are to defeat worldly ideas that obstruct the knowledge of God. In the offensive game plan you are to keep Christ in control.

This week you will learn specific ways to renew your mind by defeating worldly ideas and making every thought obedient to Christ.

"Though we live in the world, we do not wage war as the world does. The weapons we fight with are not the weapons of the world. On the contrary, they have divine power to demolish strongholds. We demolish arguments and every pretension that sets itself up against the knowledge of God, and we take captive every thought to make it obedient to Christ" (2 Cor. 10:3-5).

This week's Scripture-memory verses address renewing your mind. Write them from memory in the margin. Then describe one way you need to renew your mind.

Continuing to see myself as God sees me

Be not conformed to this world, but be transformed by the renewing of your mind then I will be able to prove what is the perfect will of God.

I urge you to give your body a living sacrifice Holy & Acceptable to God because that is my reasonable service

Learning the Worldly Christian part of the Disciple's Personality will help you visualize what you have learned about the worldly mind.

LEARNING THE DISCIPLE'S PERSONALITY

Read the section "The Worldly Christian" (p. 136) in the Disciple's Personality presentation.

On the next page begin drawing the Worldly Christian. Leave open the doors of the spirit and the flesh. Draw a big *I* in the circle. Above the circle write *The Worldly Christian.*

The World's Way
"The acts of the sinful nature are obvious: sexual immorality, impurity and debauchery" (Gal. 5:19-21).

"Put to death, therefore, whatever belongs to your earthly nature: sexual immorality, impurity, lust, evil desires and greed, which is idolatry." (Col. 3:5-7).

"Among you there must not be even a hint of sexual immorality, or of any kind of impurity, or of greed, because these are improper for God's holy people. Nor should there be obscenity, foolish talk or coarse joking" (Eph. 5:3-5).

The Spirit's Way
"The fruit of the Spirit is love, joy, peace, patience, kindness, goodness, faithfulness, gentleness and self-control. Against such things there is no law" (Gal. 5:22-23).

"Since, then, you have been raised with Christ, set your hearts on things above, where Christ is seated at the right hand of God. Set your minds on things above, not on earthly things. For you died, and your life is now hidden with Christ in God" (Col. 3:1-3).

"Be imitators of God, therefore, as dearly loved children and live a life of love, just as Christ loved us and gave himself up for us as a fragrant offering and sacrifice to God" (Eph. 5: 1-2).

Trace over the letter *s* in *spirit* with a capital *S*. Refer to the Disciple's Personality presentation (pp. 133–39) if you need help. By the end of this study you will be able to draw the complete Disciple's Personality and to explain it in your own words.

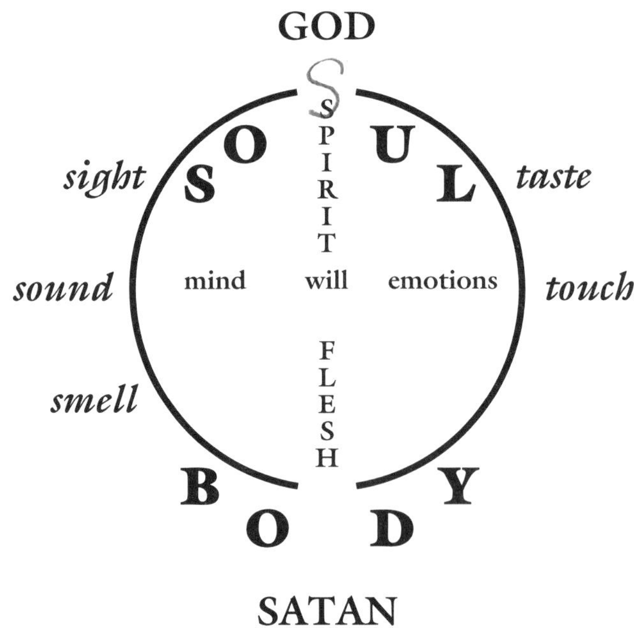

IN THE CARPENTER'S SHOP
In week 1 you learned the difference between the old person and the new person. This week you are focusing on specific ways your character can change with the help of the Holy Spirit.

Read the Scriptures in the margin that relate to immorality or impure thinking. From the verses under "The World's Way" identify a specific behavior you want to get rid of. From the verses under "The Spirit's Way" identify an action you will take to replace it. Each day this week you will record your progress in working on this trait. If you feel that this matter is too personal to write about here, you may write about it elsewhere, but please address this critical change.

Here is an example.

Behavior I want to work on: sexually impure thoughts or actions

An action I will take to put off the old self: stop looking at sexually explicit material

An action I will take to let the Holy Spirit make me more like Christ: memorize Scripture to have a pure heart and mind

Now you try it.

Behavior I want to work on: Self control eating

An action I will take to put off the old self:

Prayer before every meal.

An action I will take to let the Holy Spirit make me more like Christ:

listen, obey and follow through

THE DESIRE TO CHANGE

A word about putting off old behaviors: *in some cases you cannot change these practices overnight.* Do not be discouraged if you do not see instant results. But by asking the Lord to renew your mind and by committing this process to Him, you will eventually change. If you need a quick reference on how to renew your mind, see the chart in the margin on page 44. Feel free to copy it to keep in a convenient place.

Find a way to do something kind for a member of your family who does not know Christ. Be ready to share your experience at your next group session.

Read Ephesians 2:1-10, a passage explaining how we are made alive in Christ, in your quiet time today. Then complete the Daily Master Communication Guide in the margin.

DAY 3

Replacing Your Thoughts

Jimmie and Edna Harrison were long-time church members in West Columbia, Texas, but they found that committing every aspect of their lives to the Lord was difficult for them. Putting church ahead of work schedules was especially challenging. But when Jimmie heard about the *MasterLife* group beginning at their church, he became interested and urged Edna to study it with him. Edna went along with much reluctance.

When the group began to study about the worldly Christian and the need to renew their minds, however, the Holy Spirit began working in Edna's life, the minister reported. "She began to see herself as a worldly Christian who thought only of herself, and God began to work.

DAILY MASTER COMMUNICATION GUIDE

EPHESIANS 2:1-10

What God said to me:

____

____

____

____

____

____

____

____

What I said to God:

____

____

____

____

____

____

____

____

____

MasterLife became a joy, and she could not wait until the next week to learn more. She was a changed person."

THE MIND OF CHRIST

As a Christian, you have the goal of thinking and acting from the mind of Christ. In Philippians 2:5 Paul said, "Let this mind be in you, which was also in Christ Jesus" (KJV). He also referred to the mind of Christ in 1 Corinthians 2:16: " 'Who has known the mind of the Lord that he may instruct him?' But we have the mind of Christ" (1 Cor. 2:16).

In 1 Corinthians 2:16 what did Paul claim that Christians have?

The mind of Christ
___

Paul said that Christians have the mind of Christ. Can you sincerely say that you desire to think Christ's thoughts?
❑ Yes ❑ No

Ideally, you were able to answer yes to that question. You may sincerely desire to be Christlike and to think Christ's thoughts. But how do you do that? Renewing your mind is accomplished by filling your mind with Christ's thoughts.

Renewing your mind is accomplished by filling your mind with Christ's thoughts.

Check the phrases that explain what having the mind of Christ means.
❑ 1. Making thoughts obedient to Christ
❑ 2. Exercising the ability to think spiritually
❑ 3. Having a high IQ
❑ 4. Seeing things from Christ's viewpoint
❑ 5. Meditating to empty your mind

If you think Christ's thoughts, you try to see things as Christ would, and you let Him, not Satan, be the master of your mind. You make your thoughts obedient to Christ, and you think spiritually. Having a high IQ and emptying your mind by meditation have nothing to do with having the mind of Christ. Every Christian has the mind of Christ, but he or she does not always choose to engage it. The correct answers are 1, 2, and 4.

Every Christian has the mind of Christ, but he or she does not always choose to engage it.

Based on what you have learned so far, fill in each blank with one of the following words to describe a way Christ can be the master of your mind.

renewing thought mind knowledge

By removing all obstacles to your Knowledge___ **of God**

By making every ________________ obedient to Christ

By possessing the ________________ of Christ

By ________________ your mind

You can make Christ the master of your mind by removing all obstacles to your knowledge of God, by making every thought obedient to Christ, by possessing the mind of Christ, and by renewing your mind.

What do this week's Scripture-memory verses say about renewing your mind? Say them aloud from one to three times to continue your memory work on them. Review your memorization of Philippians 2:13 from last week.

THE RENEWAL PROCESS

To renew your mind, you begin filling your mind with Scriptures to replace bad thoughts with good thoughts. The more you live in the Word, the more your mind will be renewed.

The Scriptures in the margin give you further instruction on how Christ renews your mind. Read the verses and match the references in the left column with the summary statements in the right column.

____ 1. Colossians 3:2	**a. Think on praiseworthy things.**
____ 2. Romans 8:5-6	**b. Give attention to things of the Spirit.**
____ 3. John 16:13	**c. Let the Holy Spirit guide you into truth.**
____ 4. Psalm 1:2	**d. Set your heart's desire on heavenly things.**
____ 5. Philippians 4:8	**e. Meditate on God's Word.**

Do not let your mind linger on evil thoughts; instead, think about wholesome things, such as God's Word. Remember the computer axiom: "Garbage in, garbage out." When you realize that you are having worldly thoughts, think of them as red, flashing emergency lights that warn you to turn your thoughts to spiritual things. The correct answers are 1. d, 2. b, 3. c, 4. e, 5. a.

Here are simple, practical steps for activating the mind of Christ when you are tempted to act in harmful ways.

ACTIVATING THE MIND OF CHRIST

1. Remember that Christ was tempted in every way you are tempted yet overcame the temptation (see Heb. 4:15).
2. Pray for grace in time of need (see Heb. 4:16).
3. Express humility by getting on your knees (see Phil. 2:5-11).

"Set your minds on things above, not on earthly things" (Col. 3:2).

"Those who live according to the sinful nature have their minds set on what that nature desires; but those who live in accordance with the Spirit have their minds set on what the Spirit desires. The mind of sinful man is death, but the mind controlled by the Spirit is life and peace" (Rom. 8:5-6).

" 'When he, the Spirit of truth, comes, he will guide you into all truth. He will not speak on his own; he will speak only what he hears, and he will tell you what is yet to come' " (John 16:13).

His delight is in the law of the Lord,
and on his law he meditates day and night (Ps. 1:2).

"Finally, brothers, whatever is true, whatever is noble, whatever is right, whatever is pure, whatever is lovely, whatever is admirable—if anything is excellent or praiseworthy—think about such things" (Phil. 4:8).

Daily Master Communication Guide

Philippians 2:5-11

What God said to me:

Have My mind, have My heart and yet remain humble at all times no matter what situation you find yourself in no tha I am there.

What I said to God:

Yes God, thank you for loving me & pursuing me.

4. Adopt God's attitude and choose His response toward the temptation.
5. Ask the Holy Spirit to impress you with a way to deal with the temptation (see Prov. 3:5-6).
6. Ask for God to walk with you past the temptation.
7. Look for a Scripture to claim during the temptation.
8. Ask God to help you focus on His will (see Phil. 2:13).
9. Acknowledge and ask forgiveness for thinking about the temptation (see 1 John 1:9).
10. Obey God's commands, knowing that you are in spiritual warfare (see Rom. 8:26-27).

IN THE CARPENTER'S SHOP

What progress are you making in putting off the old self and replacing it with the new?

Yesterday you listed a behavior you wanted to reject in order to build Christlike character. Describe an instance in which you have already put aside that behavior.

Resisting ice cream 2 nights in a row even though I wanted it badly I did not go there

As you continue to put off the old self and put on new, Christlike traits, I hope that you are spending time with the Master daily. Keeping a journal, using the Daily Master Communication Guide in the margins of this book, or expanding that method in a notebook can help you examine daily what God says to you and what you say to God. In addition to my daily Bible reading, I reflect for an hour or two each week on what God has said to me that week. Each month I take a half day or a day to evaluate what God has said to me that month. Often, I realize that God has been saying something to me for a month that I became conscious of only a day or so earlier. By keeping me in touch with what God is saying to me, this practice has helped me obey Him.

Read Philippians 2:5-11 during your quiet time today. See how God speaks to you through this passage on having the mind of Christ. I hope that you are continuing to meet your goal of having quiet times 21 consecutive days. Then complete the Daily Master Communication Guide in the margin.

DAY 4

Thinking Christ's Thoughts

You may think: *Is it really possible for me—a sinful human being—to have the mind of Christ? I can imagine a well-known evangelist's being able to think Christ's thoughts, but someone like me? Isn't it presumptuous to believe that I can think as Christ does?*

YOU HAVE THE MIND OF CHRIST

Believing that you can have the mind of Christ is not presumptuous. The mind of Christ came to you when you were saved (see 1 Cor. 2:16 in the margin). God created you to be like Jesus. Romans 8:29 says, "Those God foreknew he also predestined to be conformed to the likeness of his Son, that he might be the firstborn among many brothers." Hebrews 2:10 says that God is the process of "bringing many sons to glory." The glory you are to have is the glory of being like God's perfect Son, Jesus Christ. Philippians 2:5, which you read yesterday as part of your daily Bible reading and quiet time, reminds you that you have Christ's mind. Would the Bible remind you that you have Christ's mind if engaging it and putting it to work for you were impossible? How, then, do you know how to think the thoughts of Christ? By knowing Christ, hearing Him, and learning His truth.

" 'Who has known the mind of the Lord
that he may instruct him?'
But we have the mind of Christ" (1 Cor. 2:16).

From what book can you know Christ, hear Him, and learn His truth?

____

Read John 8:31-32 in the margin or quote it from memory, having learned it in your study of *MasterLife 1: The Disciple's Cross.* What does living in God's truth do for the enslaved mind?

____

" 'If you hold to my teaching, you are really my disciples. Then you will know the truth, and the truth will set you free' " (John 8:31-32).

Living in God's Word, the Bible, is the primary source of your knowledge about Christ. The Word reveals His truth. As you hold to, or remain in, the Word, He speaks to you through the Holy Spirit. One of the Holy Spirit's roles is to show you the truth. His truth sets the enslaved mind free.

Live in His Word now by working on this week's Scripture-memory verses, Romans 12:1-2. Write them in the margin.

DAILY MASTER COMMUNICATION GUIDE

LUKE 4:14-21

What God said to me:

What I said to God:

What term did Jesus use in John 8:31-32 to describe a person who holds to, or remains in, His Word?

follower   disciple   convert   sinner

A person who holds to His Word is His disciple. These verses say that you will be His disciple indeed if you hold to, or remain in, His Word.

Having your daily quiet time is a way you continue in His Word. One goal in shaping your personality to be like Christ is to have quiet times 21 consecutive days. If you miss a day, start over. During your quiet time today read Luke 4:14-21, about a time when Jesus read from the Scriptures about His Father's will for Him. Then complete the Daily Master Communication Guide in the margin.

Use the following questions to evaluate the degree to which your mind is being renewed daily.

Are you really Jesus' disciple? ☑ Yes ❑ No If so, how do you know? Review 1 Corinthians 2:16 and John 8:31 in the margin on page 39 and state how you know that you are Christ's disciple.

By knowing the mind of Christ and holding to His teachings

If you are Jesus' disciple, what source of power renews your mind daily?

Christ - The power of God

Are you willing to commit to make God's Word a part of your daily life? ☒ Yes ❑ No If so, write a specific goal you have set for yourself.

I will Spend 5:30 time with Him.

IN THE CARPENTER'S SHOP

Does your character reveal that you have a renewed mind? What progress are you making in putting off the old self and developing a new character, with the Holy Spirit's help?

Yesterday you described a step you have taken to get rid of the old self. Today describe a new quality Christ is adding to your life.

Peace and taking away fear doubt.

PRAYING FOR CHRISTLIKE CHARACTER

One way to seek insight into building Christlike character is to ask others to pray with you about it. One of the most rewarding and effective ways to pray with others is conversational prayer. Used correctly, conversational prayer has brought genuine revival in numerous groups around the world.

Conversational prayer is a group's talking together with God. In any group conversation each person says a few sentences, and then someone else adds something to the subject. When that subject comes to a natural conclusion, someone brings up another subject. The same process takes place in conversational prayer. The following guidelines can help you experience prayer in a new, exciting way.

Read the principles of conversational prayer that follow. Draw a star beside the aspect of conversational prayer you think you will find most challenging. Ask God to help you with that aspect.

PRINCIPLES OF CONVERSATIONAL PRAYER

1. Recognize that God is in the group and that you, as a group, are conversing with Him about matters of mutual interest. Some groups even place an empty chair in their midst to remind them that He is present.
2. Pray about one subject at a time. No one should begin praying about a new subject until everyone who wants to pray about the present subject has had an opportunity. Do not be afraid of silence. You can discern when it is time to move to another subject. Do not talk about the subject; do not make lists; just pray.
3. Pray brief prayers. One or two sentences by each person on one subject are usually sufficient. This allows everyone to be involved in the conversation.
4. Speak normally. Do not use formal terms of address or a closing such as *Amen* at the end of each short prayer. Though prayed by a group, it is still one continuous prayer.
5. Use the first-person singular pronoun whenever possible: *I* and *me* instead of *we* and *us*. New Christians often do this more easily than long-term Christians do.
6. Be specific in requests and in confessions of sins. If you are specific, God helps other persons pray about the same need. One person in a group might say, "Help me with pride." Another says, "Lord, I have that problem, too." People do not recognize many answered prayers because they did not pray specifically.
7. Continue the conversation as long as the group desires or the time limit allows. Someone may have to slip out for a few minutes. Bodily position is not important. Pray with your eyes open if that is comfortable. John 11:41 implies that Jesus did. You may need to close your eyes in order to concentrate on the Lord. Let God talk to you as you talk to God.

Recognize that God is in the group.

Be specific in requests and in confessions of sins.

Pray with a friend, a family member, or your prayer partner and teach that person the principles of conversational prayer. Write a day and a time when you plan to do this:

did it Sunday c̄ Karen

Stop and ask God to help you with the challenging area beside which you drew a star in "Principles of Conversational Prayer." Ask Him to make conversational prayer a rewarding part of your life in the Spirit.

DAY 5

A Reminder of Who You Are

You truly have the mind of Christ and can think His thoughts.

This week you have learned what the Bible says about the need to renew your mind. You have learned that you truly have the mind of Christ and can think His thoughts. But how does this ability apply to you on the job, in your family life, in your church relationships, and in daily challenges?

Read the following case studies and explain how each person could renew his or her mind.

> Linda and her husband, Frank, were burdened with debt. Credit-card bills and loans kept them financially strapped. Linda and Frank both had to work two jobs to make ends meet. At the end of the day both were so tired that they had little energy to devote to their two children. Linda's weakness was catalog shopping. Anytime an appealing catalog arrived in the mail, Linda felt an overwhelming temptation to order something. When she charged the order on her credit card, she increased her family's debt even more. What could Linda do to renew her mind?

Study and meditate on scripture relating to Self-control, Proverb 31

> Tony had been without work for three months. Being unemployed made him feel embarrassed. His wife tried to maintain a supportive environment at home, but sometimes she lapsed into criticizing Tony, which made him feel even worse. During his daily run in the park, Tony encountered an attractive woman who ran at the same time he did. They started talking at the

water fountain. When he told her about his unemployment, she sympathized. Soon Tony found himself thinking more and more about this new female acquaintance and the way she encouraged him. What could Tony do to renew his mind?

Linc was involved in his church's program of evangelistic outreach. Recently, his team had experienced much success in visiting non-Christian prospects and leading them to Christ. Each week for the past five weeks one or more persons had given their hearts to Christ during one of Linc's visits. Word of these conversions spread throughout Linc's church. One day during the sermon his pastor commended Linc for his witness. Linc began to think that his success in witnessing might help him be elected chairman of the deacons. Enjoying the attention the church gave him, Linc became proud. What could Linc do to renew his mind?

You may have answered something like this:

Linda could renew her mind by recognizing her temptation and by discarding catalogs as they arrive before looking through them. She could replace thoughts of acquiring more by learning biblical teachings about material possessions and by developing a specific plan for reducing the family's debt.

Tony could renew his mind by changing his running time or place so that he will not encounter a situation that could lead him to ruin his marriage. He could pray for the Holy Spirit to show him ways to strengthen his marriage, such as spending more time with his spouse, talking honestly about their issues, and consulting a minister or a Christian counselor to help him and his spouse through this stressful period.

Linc could renew his mind by asking the Holy Spirit to help him as he reads what the Bible says about the reason Christians witness: to obey Christ, not to gain others' favor. As he reads Philippians 2:5-8, he could let the mind of Christ teach him how to be humble.

REPLACING OLD THOUGHTS

Read in the margin what the Bible says about how your thoughts shape your desires and actions. When you replace harmful thoughts with ones you know will honor Christ, your entire concept of yourself can change. If you constantly tell yourself, *I'm no good*, you may begin to act out those thoughts as a self-fulfilling prophecy. If you remind yourself of

"As he thinketh in his heart, so is he" (Prov. 23:7, KJV).

Christ's great love for you and of your worthiness in His sight, you will begin to act like a person of worth. You can renew your mind by replacing negative thoughts about yourself with the reminder that Christ died for you. You can renew your mind by remembering who—and whose—you are.

HOW TO RENEW YOUR MIND

Here is a quick reference for renewing your mind. Keep a copy in your Bible, wallet, or purse for ready access.

- **Sing songs of praise.**
- **Memorize applicable Scriptures.**
- **Pray.**
- **Bring every thought under Christ's control.**
- **Set your mind on things above.**
- **Demolish Satan's strongholds.**
- **Commit yourself to God as a living sacrifice.**
- **Talk to a friend.**
- **Help someone in need.**
- **Claim the mind of Christ.**

Describe specific situations in which you need to renew your mind.

Finances

Identify actions you will take to renew your mind. See the list in the margin for possibilities. Also review your answers, as well as the suggested answers, to the case studies you read. Some of those may apply to you.

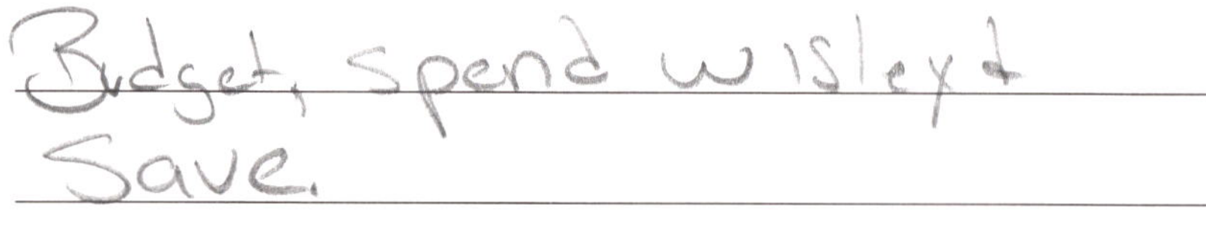

Stop and pray, asking God to give you courage to take the action you described.

Say aloud this week's Scripture-memory verses, Romans 12:1-2, to someone you think could benefit from them. Explain to that person how these verses encourage you to renew your mind.

No doubt you sometimes feel conflict in your heart when you try to have the thoughts, attitudes, and actions of Jesus. Why does such conflict arise to interfere with your commitment to have the mind of Christ? Another look at the Worldly Christian portion of the Disciple's Personality provides an answer.

"Brothers, I could not address you as spiritual but as worldly—mere infants in Christ. I gave you milk, not solid food, for you were not yet ready for it. Indeed, you are still not ready. You are still worldly. For since there is jealousy and quarreling among you, are you not worldly? Are you not acting like mere men?" (1 Cor. 3:1-3).

LEARNING THE DISCIPLE'S PERSONALITY

Read 1 Corinthians 3:1-3 in the margin. Why did Paul say that the Corinthian Christians were worldly instead of mature?

Jealousy + quarreling

Paul told the Christians at Corinth that they were not yet mature Christians because they had allowed jealousy and quarreling among them. If you do not allow Christ continually to be the Master of your life through His Spirit, you are a worldly Christian. Although you have allowed Christ to enter your life, you still struggle to control your own life. The big *I* of the old, natural person still dominates you. Worldly Christians, though children of God, continually open the door of the flesh, allowing the old nature to determine what they think, do, and feel, rather than follow the Spirit of God. You observed this situation when you read about Linda, Tony, and Linc in the case studies. You may see it in yourself, too.

The part of the Disciple's Personality drawing you learned in day 2 appears below. Write *1 Corinthians 3:1-3* under the heading *The Worldly Christian*. By the end of this study you will be able to draw the complete Disciple's Personality and to explain it in your own words.

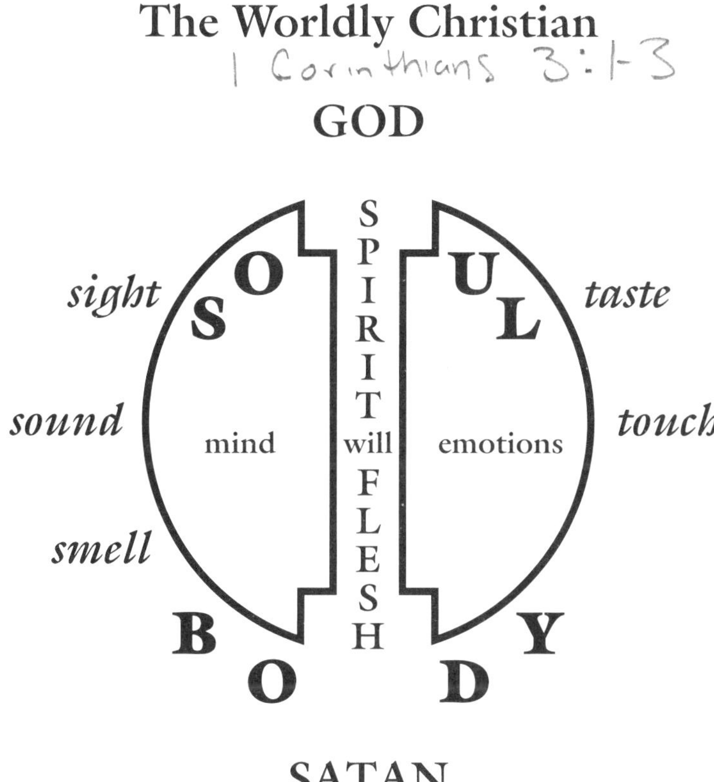

Setting aside old patterns can be challenging, but do not despair. Christ wants to be your Lord and to give you daily victory. The Holy Spirit will help you renew your mind. Week 3 will provide more positive steps to take.

Christ wants to be your Lord and to give you daily victory.

Bob Dutton, a teacher and conference leader from Hendersonville, North Carolina, became aware of the worldly lives of many American Christians when he led *MasterLife* training in the village of Krasnoyarsk Krai in Russia, once under the control of an atheistic government. Bob wept when he led these inspired Russian Christians, who had sacrificed time and possessions to travel to the training. "I was ashamed," Bob said. "I was there to help dedicated Christians learn more about the

DAILY MASTER COMMUNICATION GUIDE

GENESIS 50:15-21

What God said to me:

____

____

____

____

____

____

____

____

What I said to God:

____

____

____

____

____

____

____

____

____

Bible, and I had to admit that most Christians in America are more concerned with themselves than with following Christ. It was hard to admit that our government leaves God out of its decisions while I sat in a classroom in Siberia teaching persons who have experienced persecution and oppression."

Read Genesis 50:15-21 during your quiet time today. See how God speaks to you through this passage, which focuses on someone who replaced evil thoughts with good thoughts. Then complete the Daily Master Communication Guide in the margin.

IN THE CARPENTER'S SHOP

How have you done this week getting rid of the old self and adopting new characteristics and behaviors?

Answer these questions about the area you identified on page 35.

A characteristic or behavior I have been getting rid of this week:

Anxiety
____

Something Christ has added to my character this week:

Calmness
____

Stop and pray, thanking God for helping you in the areas you recorded. Ask Him to continue to give you the courage to make changes.

HAS THIS WEEK MADE A DIFFERENCE?

Review "My Walk with the Master This Week" at the beginning of this week's material. Mark the activities you have finished by drawing vertical lines in the diamonds beside them. Finish any incomplete activities. Think about what you will say during your group session about your work on these activities.

As a result of your study of "Renew Your Mind," I hope that you understand ways being a worldly Christian holds you back from being all God wants you to be. I hope that the Worldly Christian part of the Disciple's Personality will help you identify areas of weakness or compromise in your life in the Spirit. The ability to think Christ's thoughts is crucial to your life in the Spirit. Allowing Christ-honoring thoughts to replace worldly, fleshly thoughts is a challenge for most Christians. The Holy Spirit is with you to help you renew your mind. You do not have to be a victim of Satan's efforts to have you adopt his destructive attitudes. Satan is defeated when you push his thoughts out of your mind and replace them with those that please Christ.

WEEK 3

Master Your Emotions

This Week's Goal

You will be able to use an ACTION plan to master your emotions.

My Walk with the Master This Week

You will complete the following activities to develop the six biblical disciplines. When you have completed each activity, draw a vertical line in the diamond beside it.

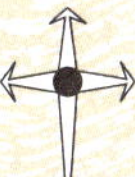

SPEND TIME WITH THE MASTER

◇ Have a quiet time each day, working toward the goal of having quiet times 21 consecutive days. Check the box beside each day you have a quiet time this week: ❑ Sunday ☑ Monday ❑ Tuesday ❑ Wednesday ❑ Thursday ❑ Friday ❑ Saturday

◇ During one day's quiet time, hold for five minutes the nail your leader gave you in your group session.

LIVE IN THE WORD

◇ Read your Bible every day. Write what God says to you and what you say to God.

◇ Memorize Galatians 5:22-23.

◇ Review Philippians 2:13 and Romans 12:1-2.

◇ Read "How to Listen to God's Word."

◇ Write important points from a sermon on the Hearing the Word form.

PRAY IN FAITH

◇ Pray for your family members and relatives.

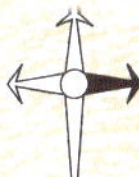

FELLOWSHIP WITH BELIEVERS

◇ Have coffee or a soft drink with someone you do not like or with a person who does not like you.

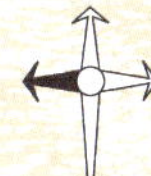

WITNESS TO THE WORLD

◇ Read "Testimony Outline" and write information to use in your testimony.

MINISTER TO OTHERS

◇ Learn the Spiritual Christian part of the Disciple's Personality.

This Week's Scripture-Memory Verses

"The fruit of the Spirit is love, joy, peace, patience, kindness, goodness, faithfulness, gentleness and self-control. Against such things there is no law" (Gal. 5:22-23).

DAY 1

A Gift from God

My father often told about having a terrible temper when he was young. Even after becoming a Christian at age 19, he often still exploded in anger. He struggled over and over again to remain calm and to have an attitude that would honor Christ.

After much prayer and Bible study my father began to notice a change in his responses to situations. One night a man stuck his fist in my dad's face and threatened him. But Dad refused to fight. He later related, "I knew I had won the battle over my temper when I did not respond as I had in the past."

Describe a situation in which your emotions got the best of you.

Last summer c̄ my husband re: his father and I opened the door so hard it put a small hole in the wall.

Almost everyone has had experiences in which controlling emotions has seemed like an overwhelming battle. In this week's study you will learn how the Holy Spirit can help you gain the victory and master your emotions.

"If it feels good, do it!" seems to be this generation's motto. This self-centered philosophy claims that your emotions are your master. Emotions make good servants but harmful masters. Christ is to be your Master, even of your emotions. He wants to help you use your emotions in a responsible way. The Bible has a plan to help you deal with your emotions. This week you will learn that plan and will understand how the Holy Spirit can help you take charge of your emotions. After this week's study you will be able to—

- relate your emotions to your values;
- list a six-step ACTION plan to deal with your emotions;
- apply the ACTION plan to an emotional experience.

WHAT ARE EMOTIONS?

Emotions are God-given feelings of pleasantness or unpleasantness. They are reactions to internal or external stimuli. Emotions are not good or bad; you make the choice of whether you use emotions to honor Christ or to harm yourself or others.

Emotions are an essential part of your personality. Life without emotions would be dull. If you did not have emotions, you would not experience anger or anxiety, but you also would not experience joy or love. God created you to experience a variety of emotions.

"He looked around at them in anger and, deeply distressed at their stubborn hearts, said to the man, 'Stretch out your hand.' He stretched it out, and his hand was completely restored" (Mark 3:5).

" 'A new command I give you: Love one another. As I have loved you, so you must love one another' " (John 13:34).

"Jesus wept" (John 11:35).

" 'I am coming to you now, but I say these things while I am still in the world, so that they may have the full measure of my joy within them' " (John 17:13).

Read the verses in the margin on the previous page and check the emotions Jesus experienced.

☑ anger ☑ love ☑ grief ☑ joy

Because Jesus was fully human, He experienced the whole range of human emotions. He experienced all of those listed. The difference between Jesus and you is that He did not sin when He experienced emotions.

THE SOURCE OF YOUR EMOTIONS

Emotions are spontaneous responses to your values and beliefs. Over the years your emotional responses have been either affirmed or challenged. Because your values and beliefs are not exactly the same as any other person's, you react to the same circumstances differently than someone else does.

During your quiet time today read Matthew 21:12-16, which describes ways Jesus used His emotions. Then complete the Daily Master Communication Guide in the margin.

Answer the following questions about Matthew 21:12-16.

The selling and buying in the temple caused different emotions in Jesus than in the chief priests and the teachers of the law. What were these emotions, and why did they experience them?

Jesus felt Anger or frustration.

Why? because of selling in the temple

The chief priests and the teachers of the law might have felt

Embarassed and ashamed

Why? Because they upset Jesus

The healing of the blind and lame man in the temple caused different emotions in the children than it did in the chief priests and the teachers of the law. What were these emotions, and why did they experience them?

The children felt thankful and ready to worship.

Why? because it showed what faith can do for those not old in their ways

The chief priests and the teachers of the law felt nothing.

DAILY MASTER COMMUNICATION GUIDE

MATTHEW 21:12-16

What God said to me:

What I said to God:

Why? Worldly Christianity

One set of circumstances can affect different persons in different ways. You may have said that Jesus felt anger because He believed that the temple should be a house of prayer, while the chief priests and the teachers of the law might have felt indifference or perhaps joy because they believed that the temple was a place where people could buy sacrifices and keep the law. They were undoubtedly enraged after Jesus drove out the money changers. You may have said that the children felt joy because people were being healed and the Messiah had come, while the chief priests and the teachers of the law felt indignant because Jesus was proclaimed the Son of David (the Messiah).

" 'A man was going down from Jerusalem to Jericho, when he fell into the hands of robbers. They stripped him of his clothes, beat him and went away, leaving him half dead. A priest happened to be going down the same road, and when he saw the man, he passed by on the other side. So too, a Levite, when he came to the place and saw him, passed by on the other side. But a Samaritan, as he traveled, came where the man was; and when he saw him, he took pity on him. He went to him and bandaged his wounds, pouring on oil and wine. Then he put the man on his own donkey, took him to an inn and took care of him. The next day he took out two silver coins and gave them to the innkeeper. "Look after him," he said, "and when I return, I will reimburse you for any extra expense you may have."

" 'Which of these three do you think was a neighbor to the man who fell into the hands of robbers?' The expert in the law replied, 'The one who had mercy on him.' Jesus told him, 'Go and do likewise' " (Luke 10: 30-37).

Analyze another Bible passage, Luke 10:30-37, in the margin. How did circumstances affect different persons in different ways?

The Levite seems to have felt indifferent. What value judgments do you think he made that produced this feeling?

Did not want to get involved.

The Samaritan evidently felt compassion and concern. What value judgments do you think he made that produced those feelings?

A true disciple

You may have answered that the Levite did not value the injured man as important or that he was in a hurry because he valued his work more than he valued the man. You may have said that the Samaritan valued the injured man enough to disrupt his plans and to contribute his resources to his healing.

Your values help determine whether you make the correct emotional response in a given situation. Too many people are glad, sad, or mad about the wrong things for the wrong reasons. If you can discern what makes you glad, sad, or mad, you can know your true values. A worldly Christian places his or her values on a self-centered life.

Think about the most recent time you were angry. Describe that experience.

Friday night ~~a~~ angry but frustrated, I chose this time to get in my car go down the street sit in a Kroger Parking lot & pray for me, and my family.

What caused this anger? Check the items that were challenged.

☑ **My position or reputation**	❑ **My plans**
❑ **My rights**	❑ **My possessions**
☑ **My identity**	❑ **My ideas**
❑ **My physical needs**	❑ **My desires**

Look again at the list and mentally check which items relate to the most recent time you felt fear, grief, joy, loneliness, anxiety, and embarrassment. Why did you feel these emotions? If you felt affirmed about the matters in the previous list, you probably experienced an emotion like joy or delight. If you felt challenged about these matters, you probably experienced fear, anger, loneliness, or betrayal. Often, a person cannot control emotions because they are narrowly focused on himself and arise from his worldly nature.

Read 1 Corinthians 3:1-3 in the margin. What did Paul call these Christians who were controlled by the emotions of jealousy and strife?

Worldly-mere infants.

"Brothers, I could not address you as spiritual but as worldly—mere infants in Christ. I gave you milk, not solid food, for you were not yet ready for it. Indeed, you are still not ready. You are still worldly. For since there is jealousy and quarreling among you, are you not worldly? Are you not acting like mere men?" (1 Cor. 3:1-3).

In previous weeks you have studied the natural person and the worldly Christian, which is what Paul called the Christians in 1 Corinthians 3:1-3. This week you will learn about the spiritual Christian, another part of the Disciple's Personality. Spiritual Christians also have strong emotions, but they have learned to master their emotions by controlling their responses to their emotions instead of letting their emotions control their responses. A spiritual Christian learns more and more to rely on the Holy Spirit instead of the flesh.

RELYING ON THE SPIRIT

Turn to page 47 and read your Scripture-memory verses, Galatians 5:22-23. What do these verses say about the Holy Spirit's role in self-control?

I will have joy, peace, patience I will be kind. I will have goodness faithfulness from those I am in relationship with I will be gentle and I will have self control.

When the Holy Spirit transforms you, He is present in your life to give you the ability to control your emotions. The Holy Spirit can even influence you as you relate to persons whom you do not particularly like or who do not like you. Sally Smith, a pastor's wife in Texas, reports that this occurred with a couple she met in *MasterLife* training in Lugansk, Ukraine. When the husband became a Christian, his wife told him that he must choose between her and God. Her father was a prominent leader in the Communist party, and she would not allow her husband to disgrace the family. As her husband struggled with his choice for about a year, great bitterness grew between the two. Finally, their

12-year-old son told his mother, "If you leave Daddy, I'm going with him." When she realized that she would lose her son, she began reading the Bible. The Holy Spirit began moving in her heart, prompting her to become a Christian and to restore the relationships with her husband and her son.

Have coffee or a soft drink with someone you do not like or with a person who does not like you. If you do not know such a person, do something for someone you do not know very well. Be prepared to share with the group what happened.

You may think: *I could never do something kind for or reach out to someone who dislikes me. If I tried, I would lose my temper.* You may not be able to, but the Holy Spirit can give you that ability by influencing you and renewing your mind. With His help, you can learn to control your emotions.

Ask the Holy Spirit to help you master your emotions and relate redemptively to others in difficult situations.

DAY 2

Taking Positive Steps

Your emotions cause you to act, but you can also act your way into an emotion.

Sometimes you may believe that your emotions are so strong that you cannot master them. You may feel that when they sweep over you like a giant tide, you have no choice but to drift along with them. However, you are not helpless in learning to control your emotions. The Holy Spirit can help you when you are tempted to give in to your emotions.

A specific course of action can help you master your emotions. It is known by the simple acrostic ACTION. Emotions are closely tied to actions. Your emotions cause you to act, but you can also act your way into an emotion. Here is what ACTION means:

A cknowledge the emotion.
C onsider why you have it.
T hank God that He will help you master it.
I dentify the biblical response to it.
O bey the Holy Spirit's leading.
N urture the appropriate fruit of the Spirit.

Over the next few days you will examine each element of this ACTION plan to learn how to deal with your emotions.

ACKNOWLEDGE THE EMOTION

The first step is to **acknowledge the emotion**. Denying or suppressing your emotions does not help. Have you heard someone shout through clenched teeth, "I am not angry!"? The words are entirely different from the emotion communicated. You can deal with an emotion only if you recognize it.

Read Matthew 26:37-38 in the margin. What was the first thing Jesus did about His grief and distress as He faced the cross?

He was sorrowful, troubled and overwhelmed.

"He took Peter and the two sons of Zebedee along with him, and he began to be sorrowful and troubled. Then he said to them, 'My soul is overwhelmed with sorrow to the point of death. Stay here and keep watch with me' " (Matt. 26:37-38).

Jesus did not try to deny or suppress His grief and distress as He faced the cross but admitted that He was sorrowful. Burying an emotion can cause it to emerge in an unhealthy way later. Suppressing emotions can make you physically ill as well as add to the emotional load you carry.

Learning to identify your exact emotion will help you acknowledge your feelings. For example, you may think you are feeling sad about a matter when a closer look reveals that you actually feel lonely, abandoned, helpless, or overwhelmed. Giving an exact name to an emotion helps with the later steps of this action plan. Try this activity to identify emotions more accurately.

Reflect on the most recent time you remember feeling a strong emotion about a matter. Check the feeling or feelings that most precisely described you at that time.

❑ **disappointed**	❑ **hopeful**	❑ **abandoned**	❑ **validated**
❑ **satisfied**	❑ **lonely**	❑ **excited**	❑ **other:**
❑ **frightened**	❑ **victorious**	❑ **embarrassed**	____________
❑ **jubilant**	❑ **helpless**	❑ **assured**	____________
❑ **betrayed**	❑ **calm**	❑ **confused**	____________

Certainly, many more feeling words than these exist to describe emotions. You may want to add to this list.

CONSIDER WHY YOU HAVE THE EMOTION

A second action step toward mastering an emotion is to **consider why you have it**. After you have acknowledged a feeling, it is important to understand why you are experiencing it. Doing this may not be as simple as you think. Sometimes an event that occurred several hours or days before is still in your subconscious, causing an emotional reaction. Try this exercise.

Identify an emotion you had recently: disappointed

Why did you feel this way? Check all appropriate responses.

- ☐ My physical condition
- ☑ What someone said to me or about me
- ☑ What someone did to me or for me
- ☐ My thoughts
- ☐ My will
- ☐ My flesh (sinful desires)
- ☐ My relationship with God
- ☐ Other: ______________________________

Identifying the underlying cause of an emotion is a big step toward mastering your reaction to that emotion.

You may have identified that you felt confused because of something someone said to you. For example, when your boss questioned whether you have the skills to do a project, you were confused because you completed training two months ago that you thought qualified you. Or maybe you identified feeling embarrassed about the physical condition of your body. Identifying the underlying cause of an emotion is a big step toward mastering your reaction to that emotion.

This week's Scripture-memory verses, Galatians 5:22-23, emphasize self-control. The verses also list characteristics you will have if the Spirit controls your life. To work on memorizing the verses, list the nine fruit of the Spirit. Check your work by referring to page 47.

✓ joy	✓ patience
✓ peace	love
gentleness	self-control
kindness	goodness
faithfulness	

Learning the next portion of the Disciple's Personality will reinforce the first two steps you have studied for mastering your emotions.

LEARNING THE DISCIPLE'S PERSONALITY

Read the section "The Spiritual Christian" (p. 137) in the Disciple's Personality presentation.

Begin drawing the Spiritual Christian portion of the Disciple's Personality. The basic diagram is drawn for you on the next page. Close the door of the flesh as you draw a cross in the center of the circle to encompass *spirit, flesh, mind, will,* and *emotions.* Write *crucified* across *flesh.* Above the circle write *The Spiritual Christian.* Refer to the Disciple's Personality presentation (pp. 133–39) if you need help. By the end of this study you will be

able to draw the complete Disciple's Personality and to explain it in your own words.

The Spiritual Christian

GOD

sight SOUL taste

SPIRIT

sound mind will emotions touch

smell

FLESH

BODY

SATAN

Read Galatians 2:20: "I have been crucified with Christ and I no longer live, but Christ lives in me. The life I live in the body, I live by faith in the Son of God, who loved me and gave himself for me" (Gal. 2:20). Can you make the statement Paul made? Write your name in the blanks in this adaptation of Galatians 2:20.

I, Shernice, am crucified with Christ and I no longer live, but Christ lives in me. The life I live in the body, I, Shernice, live by faith in the Son of God, who loved me and gave himself for me.

Write *S* beside the statements that describe the spiritual Christian.

S Puts the old self to death
S Is promised victory over the world, the flesh, and the devil
S Sets aside the lusts of the flesh
S Has the Holy Spirit dwelling in his or her personality
S Has God in control of both soul and body

A spiritual Christian sets aside old ways as though he or she has buried them. Some of those old ways may be fleshly lusts. A spiritual Christian can do this because God promises victory over Satan and over the world, the flesh, and the devil. The Holy Spirit, dwelling in this Christian's personality, gives God control of both soul and body. All five statements describe the spiritual Christian.

Daily Master Communication Guide

Galatians 2:11-21

What God said to me:

____

____

____

____

____

____

____

____

What I said to God:

____

____

____

____

____

____

____

____

____

The World's Way

"The acts of the sinful nature are obvious: sexual immorality, impurity and debauchery. ... I warn you, as I did before, that those who live like this will not inherit the kingdom of God" (Gal. 5:19-21).

"Now you must rid yourselves of all such things as these: anger, rage, malice, slander, and filthy language from your lips" (Col. 3:8).

"Do not let any unwholesome talk come out of your mouths, but only what is helpful for building others up according to their needs, that it may benefit those who listen" (Eph. 4:29).

The Spirit's Way

"The fruit of the Spirit is love, joy, peace, patience, kindness, goodness, faithfulness, gentleness and self-control. Against such things there is no law" (Gal. 5:22-23).

"You have taken off your old self with its practices and have put on the new self, which is being renewed in knowledge in the image of its Creator" (Col. 3:9-10).

"Be imitators of God, therefore, as dearly loved children, and live a life of love, just as Christ loved us and gave himself up for us as a fragrant offering and sacrifice to God" (Eph. 5: 1-2).

IN THE CARPENTER'S SHOP

Are you continuing to set aside, or tear down, the old self and to add new, Christlike traits to your character? In week 2 you identified a specific behavior you wanted to get rid of and an action you would take to replace it. This week you will look at more ways the Holy Spirit can help you become a new person in Christ.

Read the Scriptures in the margin, which relate to the improper use of language. From the verses marked "The World's Way" identify a specific behavior of this nature that you want to get rid of. From the verses marked "The Spirit's Way" identify an action you will take to replace it. I have given you an example. Each day for the rest of this week you will record your progress in working on this behavior.

Here is an example.

Behavior I want to work on: saying hateful things about others

An action I will take to put off the old self: stop being critical of my friends

An action I will take to let the Holy Spirit make me more like Christ: consciously be loving in my conversations about and to others

Now you try it.

Behavior I want to work on: more patience

An action I will take to put off the old self:

Don't be so quick to get angry

An action I will take to let the Holy Spirit make me more like Christ:

make a choice to think before I react.

In your quiet time today read Galatians 2:11-21, the passage in which Paul speaks of being crucified with Christ. Then complete the Daily Master Communication Guide on page 55.

Pray for your family members and relatives. Remember to keep a record of your prayers and answers to them on your Prayer-Covenant List (p. 143).

DAY 3

Giving Thanks in All Things

Sometimes people are unable to identify the causes of their emotions. You may have been able to check one of the feelings listed on page 53 or to write another one in the blank, but when you tried to determine the cause of it, you were clueless. Or perhaps you sense that your emotion is out of proportion to the event that caused it.

For example, you may know that you feel a deep sense of anger because your boss overlooked you in your company's awards ceremony, but you are puzzled about why a simple slight like this should evoke such strong feelings. Or you may know that you feel lonely and abandoned when a friend forgets a luncheon engagement with you, but you do not understand why you have great difficulty accepting her apology for her absentmindedness. If this is your situation, you may want to talk to your pastor or to a professional Christian counselor or participate in a Christ-centered support group that helps people understand more about their emotions.[1]

The person who reacts strongly to a boss who forgets to announce an award may learn that he or she has difficulty relating to authority figures because of a painful childhood relationship with a parent. The person who feels lonely and abandoned after an appointment falls through may still be struggling unconsciously with childhood feelings of abandonment by a relative. A person can take big steps toward mastering his or her emotions by discovering the deeper issues behind the strong feelings.

THANK GOD THAT HE WILL HELP YOU MASTER THE EMOTION

Whether or not you can identify the cause of your emotion, you can take the third action step: **thank God that He will help you master it**. Observe where this step fits into the ACTION acrostic.

Recall the key words in the first two steps in the ACTION acrostic.

A cknowledge **the emotion.**
C onsider **why you have it.**
T hank God that He will help you master it.
I dentify the biblical response to it.
O bey the Holy Spirit's leading.
N urture the appropriate fruit of the Spirit.

Read Psalm 42 during your quiet time today. Then complete the Daily Master Communication Guide in the margin.

DAILY MASTER COMMUNICATION GUIDE

PSALM 42

What God said to me:

What I said to God:

In Psalm 42 what are the action steps David took when he felt strong emotion about his sin?

Admitting he was cast down

In grief about the death of his son and about his own spiritual condition, David took action steps that are good examples for us. David admitted that he was downcast, analyzed why he felt this strong emotion, and thanked God because he believed that God would help him.

You do not have to understand a situation to believe that God will work in it and to be grateful that He will do so.

"Give thanks in all circumstances, for this is God's will for you in Christ Jesus" (1 Thess. 5:18).

Read 1 Thessalonians 5:18 in the margin. In which situations are you to give thanks?

In all circustances

"We know that in all things God works for the good of those who love him, who have been called according to his purpose" (Rom. 8:28).

Read Romans 8:28 in the margin. Why can a person of faith give thanks in everything?

In all things God works for those who love Him.

"About midnight Paul and Silas were praying and singing hymns to God, and the other prisoners were listening to them" (Acts 16:25).

Read Acts 16:25 in the margin. How did Paul and Silas prevent their situation from producing harmful emotions?

By praying & singing.

You are to give thanks in all things, not just the ones you understand or the ones that please you. If you are a person of faith, you can do this because you believe that God will work all things together for good. Paul and Silas prayed and sang hymns to keep themselves from reacting harmfully to being jailed. When by faith you trust God to work in a situation and when you thank Him for doing so, your mind is open to consider the benefits that may result.

List benefits that might result because you have the following emotions.

Fear: growth

Anger: hurting someone or yourself

Loneliness: depression

Joy: Peace

Jealousy: Financial distress

Even though you may not like to think about feeling fear, anger, loneliness, or jealousy, these emotions can have good results. Fear may keep you from taking unnecessary risks or may prompt you to take extra precautions in a situation. Anger might lead you to right a wrong or an injustice. A person who is lonely may learn to rely on God to fill the emptiness in his or her life. Jealousy can make you realize that you need to work more diligently in a relationship or to strive harder toward a goal. From joy you may reach out in kindness to others or may give praise to God for a development in your life.

Continue working on your memory verses, Galatians 5:22-23. Say them aloud to a friend. Share the way you believe the Holy Spirit is helping you learn to have self-control, the final fruit of the Spirit mentioned.

IN THE CARPENTER'S SHOP

What progress are you making in getting rid of the old self and adding new behaviors to your life?

Yesterday you identified a behavior you hoped to put away in order to build Christlike character in the way you use language. Today describe an instance in which you have acted to set aside the old behavior.

Spending time in the Word through study and prayer often helps you make progress toward putting off the old self and adding Christlike thoughts and actions to your life. Besides reading the Word, you can also receive insight by hearing the Word preached or taught. Many times insight from a preacher, speaker, or Bible-study leader is the exact tool the Holy Spirit uses to help you meet your goal.

You can receive insight by hearing the Word preached or taught.

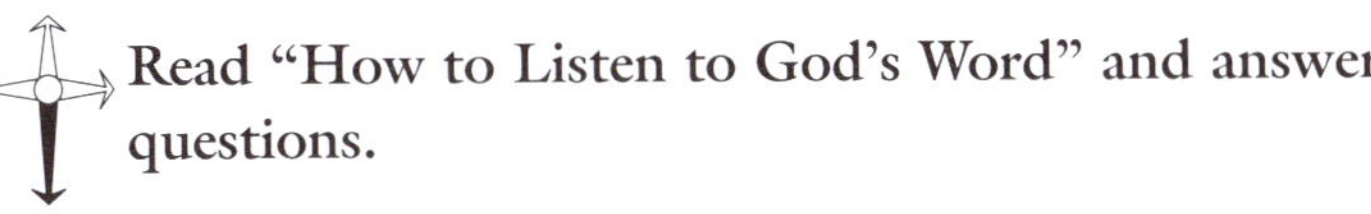

Read "How to Listen to God's Word" and answer the questions.

HOW TO LISTEN TO GOD'S WORD

1. Evaluate what kind of hearer you are. Read Matthew 13:3-23 and classify yourself as one of the following.
   a. *Apathetic hearer:* hears the word but is not prepared to receive and understand it (see v. 19).

Pay attention to what the Bible says about you, just as you would to your reflection in a mirror.

Do I let the message go in one ear and out the other?
❑ Yes ☒ No

b. *Superficial hearer:* receives the word temporarily but does not let it take root in the heart (see vv. 20-21).

Do I simply accept what is said without making specific, personal application? ❑ Yes ☒ No

c. *Preoccupied hearer:* receives the word but lets the worries of this world and the desire for things choke it (see v. 22).

Do I remember to practice the message during the week, or do I let other priorities crowd it out? ☒ Yes ❑ No

d. *Reproducing hearer:* receives the word, understands it, bears fruit, and brings forth results (see v. 23).

Does the message yield maximal fruit in my life? ☒ Yes ❑ No

2. Be alert for a word from God: "Be quick to hear" (Jas. 1:19, RSV).
3. Clear away all sin and pride so that the word can be planted in your heart (see Jas. 1:21).
4. Pay attention to what the Bible says about you, just as you would to your reflection in a mirror (see Jas. 1:23).
   a. Takes notes on the Hearing the Word form (see p. 141). List the date, place, speaker, text, and title of the message if given.
   b. Write the points of the message as the speaker presents them.
   c. Under each point write explanation, illustrations, and application. If all of these elements are not mentioned, write those that are.
   d. Write any specific statements the Spirit impresses on you.
   e. Summarize as soon as possible the main point the speaker wants you to do, be, and/or feel as a result of this sermon. Use the following questions to write your summary.
   - What did God say to me through this message? Write the specific point that you feel God wanted you to hear in the message. It may not have been what the speaker intended, but the Lord applied it to your heart.
   - How does my life measure up to this word? Look in the mirror of the word and recognize ways you fall short of what God has said. Be specific.
   - What actions will I take to bring my life in line with this word? These actions need to be specific, immediate, measurable, and attainable within a reasonable length of time.
   - What truth do I need to study further? The Lord may impress you to search the Scriptures for more information on a particular subject mentioned in the message.

5. Do the Word, and you will be blessed in what you do (see Jas. 1:25). Check yourself several times in the days that follow to determine whether you have incorporated the message into your life and have begun to bear fruit from it.

Do the Word, and you will be blessed in what you do.

Write important points from a sermon on the Hearing the Word form on page 141. Copy the form to use with all sermons.

DAY 4

A Biblical Response

The fourth step in your ACTION plan to master an emotion is to **identify the biblical response to it.** Review the steps in the plan.

IDENTIFY THE BIBLICAL RESPONSE TO THE EMOTION
Supply the key words in the first three steps you have studied.

A cKnowledg______________ **the emotion.**

C onsider______________ **why you have it.**

T hank______________ **God that He will help you master it.**

I dentify the biblical response to it.

O bey the Holy Spirit's leading.

N urture the appropriate fruit of the Spirit.

Although emotions are spontaneous, the actions they produce do not have to be. The Bible teaches that you are responsible for how you choose to let your emotions cause you to behave. You cannot escape responsibility by blaming your behavior on a negative feeling or on the person or circumstance stimulating that feeling.

Although emotions are spontaneous, the actions they produce do not have to be.

You may believe that someone wronged you or that your family background programmed you or predisposed you to act a certain way. You may think: *I can't help that I act this way. He made me angry when he criticized me.* But can someone really *make* you angry and *make* you respond improperly? Regardless of what precipitates the event, the choice of how to respond is yours. You can sin in that response, or you can choose to honor Christ. One sin does not justify another.

In the following case studies underline each person's blaming response.

Carlene worked in an office in which she felt that her coworkers constantly antagonized her and criticized her work. One day, reaching her saturation point, Carlene raged: "What about all of the wrong things you do? You're not perfect either, you know!"

Jed was reared in a home in which his father was an alcoholic and wrote bad checks. Jed did not have a role model for dependability. As an adult, Jed tried to manage his family's finances but occasionally forgot to pay the bills. When his wife expressed concern about late payments, Jed fired back: "It's all my father's fault! He never taught me how to do this! This is just the way I am!"

Wanda's father beat her, and her mother never acted lovingly toward her. As an adult, Wanda was unforgiving and refused to communicate with her parents. She told her pastor, "I hate them for the way they treated me."

In each case the individual blamed someone else for his or her wrong actions. Even though Carlene's coworkers, Jed's father, and Wanda's parents certainly sinned in their mistreatment or bad habits, Carlene, Jed, and Wanda had choices whether to sin or take responsibility for their actions.

The Bible gives principles for responding to emotions. The better you know the Bible, the more easily you can apply it to deal with all emotions.

Read the Scriptures in the margin. Write in your own words biblical responses to the following emotions.

Hate (Luke 6:27-28): Love covers a multitude, Love conquers all.

Anxiety (Phil. 4:6-7): Go to God in all things with prayer and supplication

Joy (Phil. 4:4): God gives joy. He is joy.

Anger (Eph. 4:25-26,31-32): Forgiveness quickly

" 'Love your enemies, do good to those who hate you, bless those who curse you, pray for those who mistreat you' " (Luke 6:27-28).

"Do not be anxious about anything, but in everything, by prayer and petition, with thanksgiving, present your requests to God. And the peace of God, which transcends all understanding, will guard your hearts and your minds in Christ Jesus" (Phil. 4:6-7).

"Rejoice in the Lord always" (Phil. 4:4).

"Each of you must put off falsehood and speak truthfully to his neighbor, for we are all members of one body. 'In your anger do not sin.' Do not let the sun go down while you are still angry. Get rid of all bitterness, rage and anger, brawling and slander, along with every form of malice. Be kind and compassionate to one another, forgiving each other, just as in Christ God forgave you" (Eph. 4:25-26,31-32).

Envy (1 Pet. 2:1; 1 Cor. 13:4): die to the flesh, Study the word, Love conquers

"Rid yourselves of all malice and all deceit, hypocrisy, envy, and slander of every kind. Like newborn babies, crave pure spiritual milk, so that by it you may grow up in your salvation, now that you have tasted that the Lord is good" (1 Pet. 2:1).

"Love … does not envy" (1 Cor. 13:4).

For *hate* you may have written that the biblical response is to do good to those who hate you; for *anxiety*, that you are to pray to God and not to be anxious; for *joy*, that you are to acknowledge the source of goodness; for *anger*, that you are to avoid sinning from anger and to settle matters quickly; for *envy*, that you are to lay envy aside and to love others.

Based on the Scriptures you read in the previous exercise, describe how the characters in the three case studies might have responded in a Christ-honoring way if they had sought biblical solutions for their emotions.

Carlene: Prayer, thanking God for who she is through Christ, continuing to love those who spitefully use her, and continue to do her job as ordered by God.

Jed: Acknowledge his mistakes, confront his issues and anxiety regarding finance, ask his wife for help.

Wanda: Forgive her parents, believing they were the best parents the could be, recognizing you only parent how you are taught to parent as a kid.

You might have answered something like this: Instead of turning on her coworkers in anger, Carlene could have set a Christian example by asking her coworkers to sit down with her, individually or as a group, and calmly listen to one another's concerns about work-related issues. Instead of blaming his family background and continuing the cycle of irresponsibility, Jed could have offered to take a money-management course or could have listened to audiotapes on the subject. Or he and his wife could have reached an equitable agreement about steps each would take to manage the finances. Instead of harboring bitterness toward her parents, Wanda could have prayed that the Holy Spirit would help her forgive. She might have sought the help of a professional Christian counselor or a Christ-centered support group to learn positive ways to relate to her parents despite her painful past.

Say aloud your Scripture-memory verses, Galatians 5:22-23. Choose one of the nine fruit of the Spirit and describe on the next page how you plan to use it to master your emotions. Each fruit of the Spirit is not only an emotion but also a tool for mastering your emotions.

Self control. mastering control has become a little easier since I have learned not to take things personal. that is what I have to master

HOW WOULD CHRIST RESPOND?

As you think about ways Christ would have you master your emotions, you can remember His example on the cross—the ultimate example of a person's control of emotions. Think of the ways Christ could have responded to this event: He could have raged, threatened, blamed, or scolded. He could have called on angels to protect Him. Instead, He sought God's will in His responses, even to the end. Certainly, He expressed His sorrow, as you studied in day 2. He expressed His concern for His mother. He expressed His human physical need. But the ultimate mastery occurred when He surrendered everything to God's will, even when that meant suffering and dying on the cross.

Read John 19:17-37, the passage that describes Jesus' death on the cross, during your quiet time today. See how God speaks to you. Then complete the Daily Master Communication Guide in the margin.

Also during your quiet time today hold for five minutes the nail your leader gave you in your group session. Feel and smell the nail. Press the point of the nail against your palm. Think about Christ's suffering for you and let the Holy Spirit show you the importance of Jesus' pain for you. Read aloud Galatians 2:20 as you contemplate His suffering: "I have been crucified with Christ and I no longer live, but Christ lives in me. The life I live in the body, I live by faith in the Son of God, who loved me and gave himself for me."

IN THE CARPENTER'S SHOP

If Christ is the Master of your life, you will want to be like Him—even in your language. How is the Holy Spirit helping you tear down the old self and replace old behaviors with new ones?

List a new thought or action that replaced the one you tore down in the way you use language. How are you working to put this new thought or action in place of the old?

When my husband says something or does something I disagree with depending on the severity instead of arguing or being combative I pray!

DAILY MASTER COMMUNICATION GUIDE

JOHN 19:17-37

What God said to me:

What I said to God:

DAY 5

The Higher Calling

The fifth action step is to **obey the Holy Spirit's leading.**

OBEY THE HOLY SPIRIT'S LEADING

Look at the way this step fits into the ACTION acrostic. This time I will supply the key word and will let you finish the statement.

A ______________________________.

C ______________________________.

T ______________________________.

I ______________________________.

O bey the Holy Spirit's leading.

N urture the appropriate fruit of the Spirit.

Natural and worldly persons want to do what their emotions, mind, or will tells them. In contrast, spiritual persons obey the higher call to do what the Holy Spirit reveals. Doing what God says is right, rather than what you want to do, is a conscious act of the will. Christians understand their obligations to act rightly toward others even if they do not feel like doing so. If you wait until you feel like doing right, you may find yourself excusing your failure.

Read the following accounts. Write *E* beside those that describe someone who used feelings as an excuse for irresponsibility. Write *R* beside those in which the person acted responsibly.

_____ Jim slammed on his brakes and bore down on the horn while an elderly man crept across the street. Then Jim sped away so that he would not miss the next light.

_____ When Tommy accidentally spilled his milk, his mother grabbed him and spanked him, yelling at him to be more careful.

_____ The woman tried on many pairs of shoes in the store before announcing that she really could not afford to buy any. Then she asked directions to another shoe store. The salesperson drew her a map and thanked her for stopping by.

Daily Master Communication Guide

Matthew 26:57-68

What God said to me:

____

____

____

____

____

____

____

____

What I said to God:

____

____

____

____

____

____

____

____

____

You likely recognized that the person in the last illustration—the salesperson who went the extra mile—was the only one who dealt responsibly with emotions.

Not only do your feelings influence the way you act, but the way you act also determines how you feel. You can change your feelings by changing your actions, as the adage "Act your way into a new feeling" states. Jesus' solution for many emotional responses was to command an action rather than a feeling. Read Matthew 5:24 and Matthew 7:1-2 in the margin.

" 'Leave your gift there in front of the altar. First go and be reconciled to your brother; then come and offer your gift' " (Matt. 5:24).

" 'Do not judge, or you too will be judged. For in the same way you judge others, you will be judged, and with the measure you use, it will be measured to you' " (Matt. 7:1-2).

Read 1 Corinthians 13:4-7 in the margin. When the Bible tells you to love your fellow Christians, love is described as (check one)—
❑ an emotional feeling;
❑ a way of behaving.

"Love is patient, love is kind. It does not envy, it does not boast, it is not proud. It is not rude, it is not self-seeking, it is not easily angered, it keeps no record of wrongs. Love does not delight in evil but rejoices with the truth. It always protects, always trusts, always hopes, always perseveres" (1 Cor. 13:4-7).

Love is something you do. Love manifests itself in the way you act. Acting lovingly toward someone even if you do not feel like doing so is the essence of love. The Holy Spirit can help you do this.

Read Proverbs 16:32 in the margin. This verse says that a person who remains in control of self is stronger than the strong and mightier than the mighty. A person who declines to reply in anger, conquering his or her emotions, demonstrates more strength than does a person who conquers a city.

"He that is slow to anger is better than the mighty; and he that ruleth his spirit than he that taketh a city" (Prov. 16:32, KJV).

During your quiet time today read Matthew 26:57-68, about a time when Jesus maintained self-control in a difficult situation. Then complete the Daily Master Communication Guide in the margin on page 65.

NURTURE THE APPROPRIATE FRUIT OF THE SPIRIT

The sixth action step in mastering your emotions is to **nurture the appropriate fruit of the Spirit.**

In the ACTION acrostic below write the steps you have studied.

A ____________________.

C ____________________.

T ____________________.

I ____________________.

O ____________________.

N urture the appropriate fruit of the Spirit.

Each fruit of the Spirit is more than an emotion. Each is a stable trait of character. You develop each by having a close relationship with Christ through the Holy Spirit and by growing in maturity through experience.

You develop the fruit of the Spirit by having a close relationship with Christ.

Say aloud your memory verses, Galatians 5:22-23, which mention all of the fruit of the Spirit. Then check which fruit of the Spirit you believe you most need to develop in mastering your emotions. You may check more than one.

❑ **love**	❑ **patience**	❑ **faithfulness**
❑ **joy**	❑ **kindness**	☑ **gentleness**
❑ **peace**	❑ **goodness**	☑ **self-control**

How do you plan to develop this trait or these traits of character?

Obeying the biblical response and allowing the Holy Spirit to lead me

Stop and ask God to help you develop the aspect of your character you identified. Ask Him to help you make this a meaningful part of your life in the Spirit.

Say again the verses you memorized in previous weeks, Philippians 2:13 and Romans 12:1-2.

Before your next group session apply the ACTION steps to an emotion. Write the results below. Be prepared to describe your experience to your fellow group members.

IN THE CARPENTER'S SHOP

Review the progress you have made this week in building Christlike character. How is the Holy Spirit helping you become more like Jesus in your use of pure language?

Name the behavior you have put aside this week.

List what Christ has been adding to your character this week.

Self control, discernment, peace

LEARNING THE DISCIPLE'S PERSONALITY

Review what you have learned about the Spiritual Christian portion of the Disciple's Personality. The basic diagram has been drawn for you below. Draw the elements of the spiritual Christian as you did in day 2. Label the drawing *The Spiritual Christian* and write *Galatians 2:20* under the label. Refer to the Disciple's Personality presentation (pp. 133–39) if you need help. By the end of this study you should be able to draw the complete Disciple's Personality and to explain it in your own words.

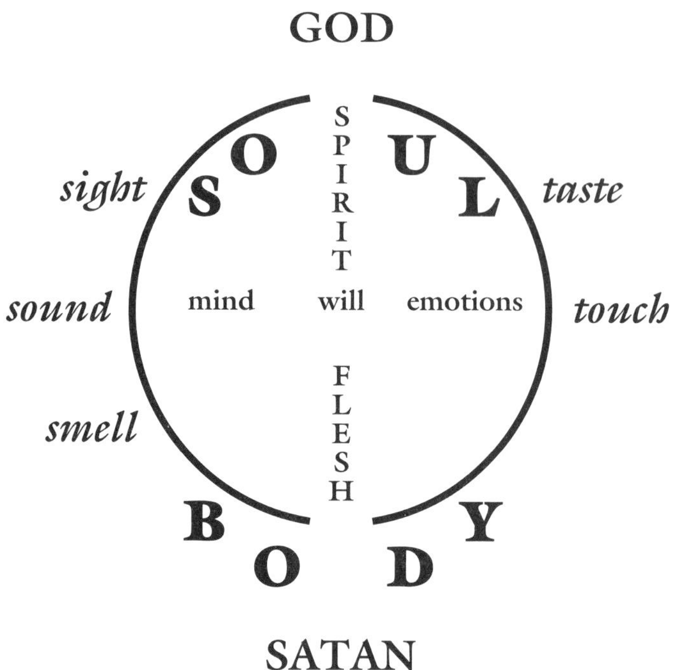

One of the most amazing stories of an individual who mastered the Disciple's Personality occurred in prison. A man named J. D., an inmate in a state penitentiary in Texas, told *MasterLife* leader Don Dennis that concepts of the Disciple's Personality now keep him from reacting violently when people make him angry.

"My old way was to react from my emotions," J. D. told Dennis, himself a former-convict-turned-preacher who pioneered using *MasterLife* in prisons. "When J. D. was in control, if someone got in my face, I would go off. I would shoot him, stab him, whatever was convenient. Part of the game I would play was to be a tough guy, a bad guy. It's one way you think you win respect, but people don't respect you. They fear you. Respect is something you get from people when you show love and kindness and consideration."

"Respect is something you get from people when you show love and kindness and consideration."

As you think about becoming a spiritual Christian and developing Christlike character, you want to share the good news. You want others to have the assurance of knowing that through Christ they can master their emotions. How do you share your joy in Christ and your assurance that the Holy Spirit will help you maintain self-control? In the next few weeks you will learn basic guidelines for writing your Christian testimony. You will develop a three-minute presentation you can share with others.

Read the following guidelines for writing your testimony. Complete the activities as you read.

TESTIMONY OUTLINE

Do you remember what the word *witness* means? It means *someone who gives evidence.* You have evidence of a changed life through the indwelling Christ. You need to verbalize that witness—to tell others who Christ is, what He has done, and how much He means to you.

A witness is someone who gives evidence.

These guidelines will help you prepare a basic testimony of your salvation experience. During the next weeks you will learn to enlarge or adapt this basic testimony to meet the needs of particular witnessing opportunities.

The apostle Paul knew how to verbalize his witness. Furthermore, he did so at every opportunity to everyone who would listen. In the margin read the words Paul wrote in Romans 1:16.

"I am not ashamed of the gospel, because it is the power of God for the salvation of everyone who believes: first for the Jew, then for the Gentile" (Rom. 1:16).

Even Christians who are skilled in giving their testimonies and in adapting their testimonies to specific situations begin with a basic testimony of conversion. And regardless of how they enlarge or adapt it, their testimonies follow a basic outline.

The Scriptures provide at least two detailed records of occasions when Paul verbalized his witness, Acts 22:1-15 and Acts 26:9-20. In both cases Paul used his conversion experience as evidence for his witness. And in both cases he mentioned four facts about it in the same order as they appear in the chart in the following activity.

Read Acts 22:1-15 and Acts 26:9-20 in your Bible. Use the following chart to analyze Paul's testimony and to identify the four necessary components of a salvation testimony. In the proper column write the references of from two to four consecutive verses from Acts 22 in which Paul told about each of four parts of his conversion experience. Then follow the same instructions when Paul verbalized his witness in Acts 26. You should be able to find each of these four components in from two to four verses, and all of these should come in the order the chart lists them. Answers appear at the end of this section.

	Acts 22	Acts 26
1. Paul had not always followed Christ.		
2. God began to deal with Paul's rebellion.		
3. Paul received Christ as his Lord.		
4. Paul's new life was centered on Christ's purposes.		

Your testimony of how you came to know Christ is personal and unique.

You may be amazed to discover that most unbelievers have never heard anyone share information of the type Paul shared in verbalizing his witness. Each conversion experience is different. Therefore, your testimony of how you came to know Christ is personal and unique. It is evidence that only you can give. No one else can duplicate it.

Although your conversion experience is unique, it can probably be outlined in much the same way Paul outlined his, especially if you became a Christian as an adult. In verbalizing your witness, share the same four types of information that Paul shared, even though the evidence itself will sound quite different.

Write four facts about your conversion that should be shared with unbelievers.

1. My life and attitudes before I followed Christ: __________

____

2. How I realized that God was speaking to me: __________

____

3. How I became a Christian: ____________________

____

4. What being a Christian means to me: ______________

____

You do not need to prepare enough material for a sermon. Witnessing is not preaching; it is giving evidence. If you can develop even a one-minute testimony of your conversion experience, you will find many opportunities to share it. In week 4 you will take the next steps in writing your testimony.

Check to see if you identified these verses on the chart of the components of Paul's testimonies: Acts 22: verses 3-5,6-9,10-13,14-15. Acts 26: verses 9-12,13-18,19,19-20.

HAS THIS WEEK MADE A DIFFERENCE?

Review "My Walk with the Master This Week" at the beginning of this week's material. Mark the activities you have finished by drawing vertical lines in the diamonds beside them. Finish any incomplete activities. Think about what you will say during your group session about your work on these activities.

As a result of your study of "Master Your Emotions" this week, I hope that you feel more confident in your ability to act in Christ-honoring ways as the Holy Spirit helps you bring your emotions under control. You may not be able to achieve the ideal results instantly. Changing old patterns takes practice. Do not be discouraged if you occasionally revert to old, out-of-control behaviors. When you do, ask forgiveness and ask God to make you aware of the Holy Spirit's presence in your life to help you make better choices.

Do not be discouraged if you occasionally revert to old, out-of-control behaviors.

[1]The following Christ-centered support-group resources are recommended to help people understand more about their emotions:
*McGee, Robert S. *Search for Significance.* Nashville: LifeWay Press, 1992.
*McGee, Robert S., Pat Springle, Jim Craddock, and Dale W. McCleskey. *Breaking the Cycle of Hurtful Family Experiences.* Nashville: LifeWay Press, 1994.
Sledge, Tim. *Making Peace with Your Past.* Nashville: LifeWay Press, 1992.
*Springle, Pat, and Susan Lanford. *Untangling Relationships.* Nashville: LifeWay Press, 1993.
*These resources are available from *www.searchlife.org.*

11/18

WEEK 4

Present Your Body

This Week's Goal

You will be able to submit your body to Christ's lordship in order to glorify God.

My Walk with the Master This Week

You will complete the following activities to develop the six biblical disciplines. When you have completed each activity, draw a vertical line in the diamond beside it.

SPEND TIME WITH THE MASTER

◇ Have a quiet time each day, working toward the goal of having quiet times 21 consecutive days. Check the box beside each day you have a quiet time this week: ❑ Sunday ❑ Monday ❑ Tuesday ❑ Wednesday ❑ Thursday ❑ Friday ❑ Saturday

LIVE IN THE WORD

◇ Read your Bible every day. Write what God says to you and what you say to God.

◇ Memorize 1 Corinthians 6:19-20.

◇ Review Philippians 2:13, Romans 12:1-2, and Galatians 5:22-23.

◇ Write important points from a sermon on the Hearing the Word form.

PRAY IN FAITH

◇ Pray that you will have victory every day with Christ.

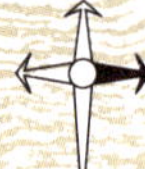

FELLOWSHIP WITH BELIEVERS

◇ Tell a Christian friend how you began to prepare your testimony in week 3. Explain what you wrote in the outline and how you plan to expand it.

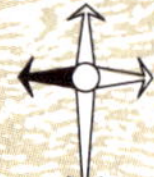

WITNESS TO THE WORLD

◇ Work on your written testimony, using the ideas in "Guidelines for Writing Your Testimony."

MINISTER TO OTHERS

◇ Learn the Steps to Victorious Living and Who Are You? parts of the Disciple's Personality.

This Week's Scripture-Memory Verses

"Do you not know that your body is a temple of the Holy Spirit, who is in you, whom you have received from God? You are not your own; you were bought at a price. Therefore honor God with your body" (1 Cor. 6:19-20).

DAY 1

Surrendering Yourself to God

When I was a missionary in Indonesia, I heard Bill Tisdale, a missionary from the Philippines, speak on surrendering the body to the Lord. He said:

You can take every member of your body and present it to Christ for His use.

> *Sometimes we have a problem surrendering ourselves to God. We try to surrender our spirits to God, and we tell God that we want to dedicate ourselves to Him. Here is a simple way to present the members of your body one by one to Christ for His use. You can say: "Lord, here are my eyes. I want to give them to You. I want them to see only the things you want them to see. Help me always look at the things You want to look at and avoid the things You do not want to look at. Here are my hands. I present them to You. Work through my hands to do what You want to do. I do not want to use my hands just for me anymore. I want You to use my hands. Here are my feet. Guide them to go where You want them to go. I give You the lordship of my body." You can take every member of your body and present it to Christ for His use.*

That illustration helped me with my difficulty in presenting my body to Christ as a living sacrifice through which He could work. Each time I was tempted to let a part of my body dominate me, I offered that part of my body to Christ so that He could master it and use it for His glory.

The stomach is a means He has provided for me to live but not indulge, so He can help me control my eating. James 3:6, in the margin, says that the tongue is a wildfire, but if I present it to God, I do not say anything He does not want me to say. I bite my tongue so that I do not say the wrong things. If I give my ears to God, I decide to listen to what honors Him.

"The tongue also is a fire, a world of evil among the parts of the body. It corrupts the whole person, sets the whole course of his life on fire, and is itself set on fire by hell" (Jas. 3:6).

Is your body or the way you feel about it mastering you?

When you look in the mirror, does what you see make you—

❑ glad? ❑ sad? ❑ mad?

Today you will consider the relationship of your physical body to your spiritual life. At the end of this week's study you may be able to answer the previous question differently. When you have completed this week's work, you will be able to—

- list three functions of the body in the human personality;
- write three facts about the nature of your body;
- distinguish between the body and the flesh;

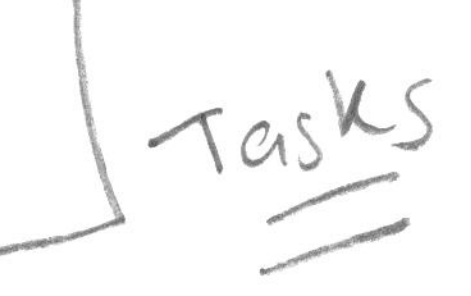

- apply Christ's incarnation, crucifixion, and resurrection to your use of your body;
- explain how to use your body for God's glory.

"The Lord God formed the man from the dust of the ground and breathed into his nostrils the breath of life, and the man became a living being" (Gen. 2:7).

GOD'S INTENTIONS FOR YOUR BODY

God created Adam's body from the dust of the earth (see Gen. 2:7 in the margin). God intends for the body to perform three essential functions:

1. Identification as a unique person—the way you look
2. Participation in the world—the way you act
3. Communication with others—the way you relate to others

Without a body you would have no contact with the physical world.

Give an example of how your body enables you to be involved in the world through each of the three functions.

1. Identification as a unique person: I don't Know. because I often hear you look like... although since loosing weight...

2. Participation in the world: By doing what God has purposed for me

3. Communication with others: By walking in Gods light + love.

You may have answered something like this: 1. No one is exactly like me. The way I look makes it possible for others to identify me. 2. I can experience the world, and I can do God's business. 3. Talking and body language are important in spreading the gospel.

Your body allows you to influence the created order. Because you have mobility, you can move from place to place to perform God's tasks. Because you have strength in your body, you can accept assignments for Him.

"God created man in his own image, in the image of God he created him; male and female he created them. God blessed them and said to them, 'Be fruitful and increase in number; fill the earth and subdue it. Rule over the fish of the sea and the birds of the air and over every living creature that moves on the ground' " (Gen. 1:27-28).

After reading Genesis 1:27-28 in the margin, list three verbs that tell three *different* things God intended for human beings to do in the world.

fruitful, subdue and rule

God expected you to be fruitful and multiply, to subdue the earth and make it useful, and to master or have dominion over living creatures. Your body makes you feel at home in the created order.

How do your body's three functions help you do what God asks you to do in relating to the world?

Identification—the way you look: By having a positvie (look) Hterly

Participation—the way you act: By shawing love and applying Godsword.

Communication—the way you relate to others: Love in spite of.

Here are possible answers: Because of identification—the way I look—someone may be attracted to my unique identity and may want to get acquainted. If we fall in love and God leads us to marry, we form a family to which children may be born. Participation—the way I act—gives me dominion over other creatures and the ability to be on mission with God in the world. Communication—the way I relate—makes it possible for me to lead, make decisions, and communicate them.

Turn to page 72 and read aloud this week's Scripture-memory verses, 1 Corinthians 6:19-20. How does God intend for you to regard your body?

Honoring God with my body

God intends for you to have a high regard for your body because it is the dwelling for His Spirit. You likely want to provide only the best dwelling for the Spirit of God.

Being disciplined is not in my nature. I have found that Spirit-control, not self-control, makes the difference. The Holy Spirit can control what I cannot control. I say again and again, "Lord, I can't control this; will You control it?" Then He takes over and controls the part of my life that my physical body might lead me to misuse or misapply.

Stop and ask the Holy Spirit to work in your life so that you have victory every day with God—in the control of your body and in other areas that come to mind.

IN THE CARPENTER'S SHOP

One way to gain control over your body is striving to change your character. The Holy Spirit can help change your character when you are in Christ. How are you working to put off the old person and to put on the new?

Daily Master Communication Guide

James 3:1-12

What God said to me:

What I said to God:

The World's Way
"Do not be foolish, but understand what the Lord's will is. Do not get drunk on wine, which leads to debauchery" (Eph. 5:17-18).

"The acts of the sinful nature are obvious: sexual immorality, impurity, and debauchery. ... I warn you, as I did before, that those who live like this will not inherit the kingdom of God" (Gal. 5:19-21).

"Put to death, therefore, whatever belongs to your earthly nature: sexual immorality, impurity, lust, evil desires and greed, which is idolatry" (Col. 3:5).

The Spirit's Way
"Instead, be filled with the Spirit" (Eph. 5:18).

"Live by the Spirit, and you will not gratify the desires of the sinful nature" (Gal. 5:16).

"Since, then, you have been raised with Christ, set your hearts on things above, where Christ is seated at the right hand of God. Set your minds on things above, not on earthly things. For you died, and your life is now hidden with Christ in God" (Col. 3:1-3).

Read the Scriptures in the margin that relate to abusing the body. From the verses marked "The World's Way" identify a specific behavior you want to get rid of. From the verses marked "The Spirit's Way" identify an action you will take to replace it. I have given you an example. Each day this week you will record your progress in working on this behavior. If this matter is too personal to write about here, you may write about it elsewhere, but please address this critical change.

Here is an example.

Behavior I want to work on: drinking substances that are harmful to me as a way of dealing with emotional pain

An action I will take to put off the old self: inquire about a support group that helps persons overcome alcohol dependency

An action I will take to let the Holy Spirit make me more like Christ: face my pain and rely on Christ's power to help me through difficult issues

Now you try it.

Behavior I want to work on: eating even smaller portions

An action I will take to put off the old self:

Be more conscious of my habits

An action I will take to let the Holy Spirit make me more like Christ:

Say a small prayer before every meal relating to portion size

Read James 3:1-12, which discusses the power of the tongue, in your quiet time today. Then complete the Daily Master Communication Guide in the margin on page 75.

How are you progressing in writing your testimony? Preparing your testimony and the encouragement of your *MasterLife* group can help you become bolder in your efforts to witness. Tell a Christian friend how you began to prepare your testimony in week 3. Explain what you wrote in the outline and how you plan to expand it.

DAY 2

Doing Things Your Own Way

In day 1 you learned that God had a plan for humankind to follow in the use of the body. He intended for people to replenish the earth, subdue it, and rule it. But the first human beings failed to do what God asked. Instead of being partners with God in ruling the world, they selfishly decided to do things their own way. The result was chaos. The good bodies of those people were invaded by a sinful nature.

What is another word for *body* that also means *the sinful nature*?

The words translated *flesh* in the Bible have two distinct meanings: *the physical body* and *the sinful nature*.

WHAT GOD EXPECTS

God created the physical body to be good, but when people sinned, the body was affected. Although the body itself is not evil in itself, it is weak and susceptible to the flesh (the sinful nature). God expects you to honor Him through your physical body and to decline to let the flesh, or the sinful nature, take over. The body has the capacity to do good if the flesh is not in control.

Read in the margin the Scriptures that show the possibility of using the body for good. Then match the references with the summary statements below.

B 1. Genesis 1:31	**a. Jesus compared His church to His body.**
D 2. John 1:14	**b. Human bodies were created as good and were pleasing to God.**
C 3. Romans 8:23	**c. Your body will be redeemed.**
A 4. Ephesians 1:22-23	**d. Jesus was incarnated in a human body.**

Your body can be used for good. The fact that Jesus was incarnated in a human body testifies to the fact that God looked with favor on the physical body. You will not always have this body but will someday redeem it for a form that Jesus wants you to have in heaven. The correct answers are 1. b, 2. d, 3. c, 4. a.

You have studied three facts about the nature of your body. Write what the following statements mean to you.

"God saw all that he had made, and it was very good. And there was evening, and there was morning—the sixth day" (Gen. 1:31).

"The Word became flesh and made his dwelling among us. We have seen his glory, the glory of the One and Only, who came from the Father, full of grace and truth" (John 1:14).

"Not only so, but we ourselves, who have the firstfruits of the Spirit, groan inwardly as we wait eagerly for our adoption as sons, the redemption of our bodies" (Rom. 8:23).

"God placed all things under his feet and appointed him to be head over everything for the church, which is his body, the fullness of him who fills everything in every way" (Eph. 1:22-23).

1. God created the body as good.

God did not intend for us to be burdened c̄ sickness + disease

2. Something happens to the body when flesh takes over.

When we give in to our fleshly desires there are great consequences.

3. God created the body for His use.

Glorify God w/ my entire physical body.

You may have responded in ways similar to this: 1. Because God created my body as good, He expects me to take care of it. 2. Because I have sinned, my body is susceptible to the ways of the flesh, and I must be on guard against the domination of worldly ways. 3. God can do anything, even use my weak body for His good.

To review what you learned earlier, list the three functions your body performs that involve you in the world.

Identification my uniqness

PARTICIPATION in the world

Communication c̄ others

If you had difficulty recalling the three functions, refer to yesterday's lesson.

IN THE CARPENTER'S SHOP

What progress are you making in allowing the Holy Spirit to help you put off the old self and replace it with the new?

Yesterday you identified a behavior you hoped to put away in order to build Christlike character. Describe an instance in which you have set aside that behavior.

Daily every meal.

You grow in your faith when you learn to give your Christian testimony.

One way to keep your body from being susceptible to un-Christlike ways is to know who you are in Christ, to stand firm in that identity, and to share your convictions with others. You grow in your faith when you learn to give your Christian testimony. Last week you began to draft a basic testimony. Yesterday you were to discuss with a friend your basic testimony and your ideas for expanding it. Today you will receive specific help for writing your testimony.

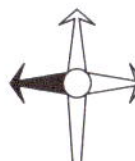 **Read the following guidelines for writing your testimony.**

GUIDELINES FOR WRITING YOUR TESTIMONY

As you become more skilled at witnessing, various situations will call for you to give your testimony differently. You will use a variety of sentences each time you give your testimony. Because each situation will be unique, your testimony will be unique to each situation.

Your testimony will probably always include the four points that you used to develop your basic testimony last week. But a particular situation may call for you to say more about one point than the others. Or you may discover that the person to whom you are witnessing identifies more closely with different illustrations and examples.

This material will prepare you to write an improved, expanded version of the basic testimony you have already developed. You will learn how to gather background material for each point in your testimony to use as needed in specific witnessing opportunities.

Find the basic testimony you have written and place it where you can see it. Write each heading on a separate sheet of paper. Make notes on each sheet as you study the following material. Your goals are to—

- be certain you said everything you needed to say about each part of your testimony;
- develop background information for adapting or emphasizing each part of your testimony when the occasion calls for it.

My Life and Attitudes Before I Followed Christ

When you tell what your life was like before you became a Christian, do not make all of it sound bad. Share the good things as well as the bad. This allows others to identify with what you say.

Share interesting details about yourself that will make you come across as an ordinary person. Be prepared to talk about—

- where you lived before you became a Christian;
- what you did before you became a Christian;
- your interests and hobbies before you became a Christian;
- your priorities before you became a Christian.

Share details about your life indicating that you truly needed greater meaning and purpose or the ability to overcome failings. Some examples are temper, habits, greed, and self-centeredness. Your purpose is not to confess your evil life but to tell your story.

Share details about your life indicating that you truly needed greater meaning and purpose or the ability to overcome failings.

Daily Master Communication Guide

Acts 16:25-34

What God said to me:

____

____

____

____

____

____

____

____

What I said to God:

____

____

____

____

____

____

____

____

How I Realized That God Was Speaking to Me

Explain how God began to show you His love while you were still an unbeliever. Be general enough for a person to identify with your description. How, when, and where did God get through to you? What person(s) did He use? Did He use a book, a film, or a Scripture? Did He shape events to speak about His waiting presence?

How I Became a Christian

Share how you trusted your life to Christ. Let the Bible be your authority rather than what someone said to you: "Here is a Bible verse that made me realize what Jesus did for me: ..." Be sure to state that you prayed to receive Christ.

You might be inclined to use "church language" here. Be sensitive to those who will not understand the meanings of such words. Also be sensitive to the fact that the person may have been frightened away by high-pressure tactics or by a zealous but tactless witness.

Make short statements about four important facts:

- Sin is an I-controlled life. It is failing or refusing to be what God wants you to be.
- Sin's penalty is separation from God both in this life and in the life to come for eternity.
- Christ paid the penalty for sin when He took your sin to the cross, accepted the judgment for it, and made it possible for you to be accepted by the Father.
- Receiving Christ is acknowledging to Him that you are a sinner, accepting forgiveness from Him, inviting Him to enter your life as your Savior and Lord, and trusting Him to do for you the things you could never do for yourself.

Check your testimony to be certain you have at least one sentence about each of these facts.

What Being a Christian Means to Me

Be careful not to give the impression that becoming a Christian automatically solved all of your problems. Describe your lifestyle as a Christian. You may not realize how different your lifestyle is from that of an unbeliever. Many things you take for granted will be significant to a non-Christian. Describe the changes that have taken place in your life in the following areas.

- Relationships with family
- Use of money
- Purpose of life
- Attitude toward death
- Value of Christian friends
- How you deal with problems, frustration, and failure

Suggestions for Giving Your Testimony

1. Keep it short so that your listener will not become uncomfortable.
2. Tell what happened to you. It is your story that others want to hear. Do not say "you"; say "I" and "me."
3. Avoid negative remarks. Do not criticize religious groups or a specific church.
4. Ask yourself, *If I were an unbeliever, what would this mean to me?*
5. Eliminate religious words. Lost persons do not understand religious jargon like *repented, made a decision for Christ, invited Jesus into my heart, walked the aisle, joined the church, saved,* and *was baptized.*

If You Accepted Christ When You Were a Child

If you were reared in a Christian home and accepted Christ as a child, do not feel that your conversion is not dramatic enough to share. It is *always* significant for an unbeliever to learn the way God enters human lives.

Read Acts 16:25-34, the passage in which Paul and Silas witnessed to the jailer, in your quiet time today. Then complete the Daily Master Communication Guide on page 80.

DAY 3

Who Is the Master of Your Body?

An award-winning athlete spent much of his spare time working with handicapped young people. A newscast showed this athlete helping physically challenged individuals. A few seconds later in the newscast another athlete was reported to have used his strong body in a harmful way. I feel sad when I hear that a successful athlete has been arrested on drug charges or has violated the law in another way.

THE STRUGGLE FOR CONTROL

The potential for your body to be used in positive, Christ-honoring ways is tremendous. However, in reality, your body is still subject to sin and death.

Read Romans 7:18-23 in the margin. Describe an experience in which you desired to do good yet did the opposite.

By overeating and then feeling emotionally and physically sick.

"I know that nothing good lives in me, that is, in my sinful nature. For I have the desire to do what is good, but I cannot carry it out. For what I do is not the good I want to do; no, the evil I do not want to do—this I keep on doing. Now if I do what I do not want to do, it is no longer I who do it, but it is sin living in me that does it. So I find this law at work: When I want to do good, evil is right there with me. For in my inner being I delight in God's law; but I see another law at work in the members of my body, waging war against the law of my mind and making me a prisoner of the law of sin at work within my members" (Rom. 7:18-23).

You may have answered something like this: I know that I hurt my children when I speak harshly to them, but I keep doing it. I know that overeating is not good for me, but I do it in spite of my good intentions.

As you became aware when you did the previous exercise, the flesh tends to use the senses and the normal desires of your body to master you. Check the pursuits that have become your masters at one time or another:

❑ food	❑ sex	❑ work
❑ money	❑ sports	❑ clothing
❑ religion	❑ others' approval	❑ beauty
❑ television	❑ education	❑ recreation

❑ **other:** ____

____

Were you surprised to see *religion* in the list? Did you think that pursuing religious matters is a way to honor Christ? Certainly, attending church and involving yourself in the fellowship of believers are what Christ intends as part of a disciple's disciplined life. Sometimes, however, your desire to be very active in your church can be motivated by harmful reasons. You may do so to obtain others' approval. You can become enslaved by this worldly desire, forgetting that God calls you to serve from obedience to Him.

"What the law was powerless to do in that it was weakened by the sinful nature, God did by sending his own Son in the likeness of sinful man to be a sin offering. And so he condemned sin in sinful man" (Rom. 8:3).

"We know that our old self was crucified with him so that the body of sin might be done away with, that we should no longer be slaves to sin—because anyone who has died has been freed from sin" (Rom. 6:6-7).

"If the Spirit of him who raised Jesus from the dead is living in you, he who raised Christ from the dead will also give life to your mortal bodies through his Spirit, who lives in you" (Rom. 8:11-13).

Read the verses in the margin. Write three primary actions Christ took to free you from bondage to the flesh.

Christ's ____________________ condemns sin in the flesh (Rom. 8:3).

Christ's ____________________ frees you from the bondage of the body of sin (Rom. 6:6-7).

Christ's ____________________ gives you life through the Spirit so that you can put to death the deeds of the body (Rom. 8:11-13).

Christ's coming to earth as a human being—His incarnation—condemns sin, His crucifixion frees you from sin's bondage, and His resurrection gives you life through the Spirit. The Holy Spirit takes these three actions of Christ and makes them real in your life. Life in the Spirit applies that work of Christ to your life.

Continue working on this week's Scripture-memory verses, 1 Corinthians 6:19-20, by saying them aloud. Check commitments you will make to honor Christ with your physical body.

I will—
- ❑ watch my intake of empty calories that do not add to my nutrition; - done
- ❑ begin an exercise program; done
- ❑ increase the amount of rest I get each day; done
- ❑ examine my eating patterns and find an alternative approach when I realize that I am eating from anxiety or tension rather than from hunger; done
- ❑ monitor my intake of substances like caffeine that do not nourish me and may make me irritable; done
- ❑ stop using substances such as nicotine, alcohol, or other drugs that harm my body. done

IN THE CARPENTER'S SHOP

In the previous exercise you checked commitments you will make. Was one of these commitments similar to the step you described yesterday to get rid of a behavior? Today describe what Christ is adding to your life to replace that part of your old self.

Yes ______________________________

____

You may be interested in noting how many sermons you hear in the next few weeks focus on honoring Christ with your body instead of allowing fleshly, sinful concerns to take control. Begin paying particular attention to encouragement you receive from sermons about this matter.

Continue to use the Hearing the Word form on page 141 to take notes on sermons. Especially note any sermon references that address the subjects you are studying this week.

In your quiet time today read Judges 16:15-30, about an Old Testament character who used his body for both good and evil. Then complete the Daily Master Communication Guide in the margin.

Daily Master Communication Guide

JUDGES 16:15-30

What God said to me:

____

____

____

____

____

____

____

____

What I said to God:

____

____

____

____

____

____

____

____

____

DAY 4

Useful to the Master

What positive steps can you take when you find yourself doing things that are the opposite of what you know is right? How can Christ master your body so that it is useful to Him in the world? You can apply to your everyday life the three actions Christ took for your salvation.

To review, list the three actions you learned in day 3.

I ~~dentification~~ incarnation.

C ~~ommunication~~ rucifixion

R essurrection

Christ's incarnation condemns sin, His crucifixion frees you from sin's bondage, and His resurrection gives you life through the Spirit.

Say aloud this week's Scripture-memory verses, 1 Corinthians 6:19-20. How does Christ's incarnation in you through the Holy Spirit apply to your body?

My body is a temple where Christ dwells and it must, it commands God's Glory

You may have written something like this: The Holy Spirit lives in me. I am God's, and my body exists to glorify God. I can use my body for His purposes.

Christ's incarnation—His coming to earth as a human being—led to His crucifixion. Christ was crucified for you.

Read the verses in the margins on this page and the next. Answer this question about each: How does your acceptance of Christ's crucifixion as the substitute for your crucifixion apply to your body?

"We know that our old self was crucified with him so that the body of sin might be done away with, that we should no longer be slaves to sin" (Rom. 6:6).

1. Romans 6:6: Our old man was crucified with Christ.

2. Colossians 3:3-4: I died & my life is ~~m~~ now in Christ

3. Galatians 5:24-25: I have crucified my sinful nature and its desires

"You died, and your life is now hidden with Christ in God. When Christ, who is your life, appears, then you also will appear with him in glory" (Col. 3:3-4).

"Those who belong to Christ Jesus have crucified the sinful nature with its passions and desires. Since we live by the Spirit, let us keep in step with the Spirit" (Gal. 5:24-25).

You may have responded this way: 1. Because my old self was crucified with Christ, I am no longer a slave to the body of sin. I am a new creature in Christ and can act accordingly. 2. Because I have died with Christ, I am to consider my bodily members dead to the deeds of the flesh (or I am to put to death the deeds of the flesh). 3. My sinful nature, with its lusts and desires, has been put to death; so I can walk in the Spirit as He directs my thoughts and actions.

Paul said, "If we died with Christ, we believe that we will also live with Him" (Rom. 6:8). Christ rose and gave you new birth.

INSTRUMENTS OF RIGHTEOUSNESS

Read Galatians 2:20 and Romans 6:11-14 in the margin. How does your participation in Christ's resurrection through the new birth and His living in you apply to your body?

I have been crucified with Christ and I no longer live, but Christ lives in me. The life I live in the body, I live by faith in the Son of God, who loved me and gave himself for me" (Gal. 2:20).

"In the same way, count yourselves dead to sin but alive to God in Christ Jesus. Therefore do not let sin reign in your mortal body so that you obey its "evil desires. Do not offer the parts of your body to sin, as instruments of wickedness, but rather offer yourselves to God, as those who have been brought from death to life; and offer the parts of your body to him as instruments of righteousness. For sin shall not be your master, because you are not under law, but under grace" (Rom. 6:11-14).

1. Galatians 2:20: Because my flesh is subject to the things of God, I live by faith

2. Romans 6:11-14: I am alive to God through Jesus and therefore I can't let sin reign in my mortal body.

You may have responded something like this: 1. The life I now live is not my own but Christ's. He reigns in my body. 2. I am alive to God. I will let Him reign in my body by yielding members of my body to Him as instruments of righteousness instead of letting them be instruments of wrong living.

Your body will not be perfect until it is completely redeemed at Christ's return. In the meantime your identification with Christ's incarnation, crucifixion, and resurrection gives you potential for righteous living. You still have potential for unrighteous living. The Scriptures you have studied urge you to put to death the deeds of the flesh.

How often does Christ expect you to take up your cross? Daily

How, then, can you live victoriously as you take up your cross daily? Through the Disciple's Personality presentation you have learned how to let God take control of your mind, your will, your emotions, and therefore your soul and body. Today you will learn another part of the Disciple's Personality presentation, Steps to Victorious Living.

Daily Master Communication Guide

John 20:1-18

What God said to me:

What I said to God:

LEARNING THE DISCIPLE'S PERSONALITY

Read the section "Steps to Victorious Living" (p. 137) in the Disciple's Personality presentation.

On the Disciple's Personality illustration below write the components of the spiritual Christian as you learned to do in week 3. Then write *Philippians 2:13* under *will, Ephesians 5:18* above *Spirit, Romans 12:2* under *mind, Galatians 5:22-23* under *emotions, Romans 6:12-13* under *flesh, 1 Corinthians 6:19-20* on one side of the circle, and *Romans 12:1* on the other side. All but two of these Bible verses have been memory verses in this study. Those two will be your memory verses in weeks 5 and 6. Refer to the Disciple's Personality presentation (pp. 133–39) if you need help. By the end of this study you should be able to draw the complete Disciple's Personality and to explain it in your own words.

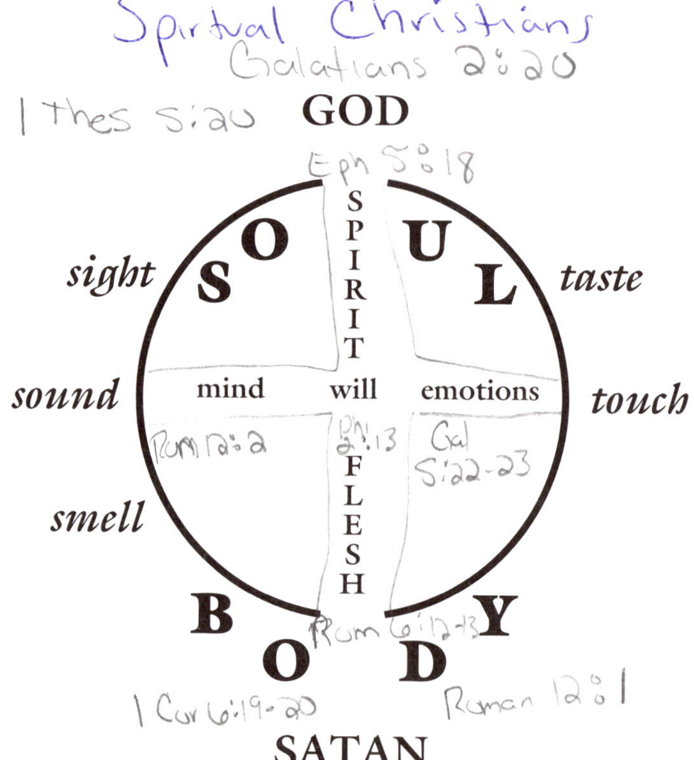

Read John 20:1-18, the passage that describes Jesus' resurrection, during your quiet time today. See how God speaks to you through this passage. Then complete the Daily Master Communication Guide in the margin.

DAY 5

A Living Sacrifice

Romans 12:1 says that you are to present your body as a living sacrifice. What does that mean? Think about the days before Christ when people presented animal sacrifices. Christ came to change that practice when He died on the cross as the ultimate sacrifice. Christ wants you in His service not as a dead sacrifice but as a living one. He wants not material things sacrificed but lives sacrificed on the altar of service to Him. He does not want a life half lived. He wants a life fully invested in Him.

Christ wants a life fully invested in Him.

If you present your body as a living sacrifice, what does that mean you will do?

Glorify God at all times with my Body

You might have answered: If I present my body as a living sacrifice for the Master's use, it means that I will be more than a Christian in name only. It means that I will do more than give lip service to my faith. I will sacrifice every area of my life to Him and will commit my body to holy, righteous living.

COMMITTING TO CHRIST'S SERVICE

In day 1 I told you about missionary Bill Tisdale, who regularly prayed a prayer committing every part of His body to Christ's service. Will you do that, too?

Write how you will use each part of your body as you present it to God for His glory.

Hands:

Eyes:

Feet:

Stomach: ______________________________

____

Sex organs: ______________________________

____

Ears: ______________________________

____

Tongue: ______________________________

____

Draw a star beside the area in which you feel you need the most help in surrendering to God.

Stop and ask God to help you remove barriers to surrendering that member of your body to the Master's service. Ask Him to help you by making you aware of the Holy Spirit's presence when you are tempted to use that part of your body in wrong living.

In day 1 you learned that God intended for you to use your body for three functions:

- Identification as a distinct personality
- Participation in the world
- Communication with others

Write one way you will commit to use your body for each of these functions in God's service.

Identification as a distinct personality: ______________________________

____

Participation in the world: ______________________________

____

Communication with others: ______________________________

____

With the relationship of your body and your spiritual life in mind, answer this question: If you were to present your body as a living

sacrifice for God's glory, how would your body make you feel?
❑ glad ❑ sad ❑ mad

Presenting your body to God can be the most freeing, gratifying, and joyful feeling in the world. You have a choice about how your body responds to situations. Recall that in the illustration of the Disciple's Personality, your will is located in a position to decide between the spirit and the flesh. If you choose to close the door of the flesh, the door will close. The decision to present your body as a living sacrifice means that you close the door of the flesh. With the Holy Spirit's help, you can change harmful habits and yield all of your life, not just part of it, to the Master.

With the Holy Spirit's help, you can change harmful habits and yield all of your life, not just part of it, to the Master.

Will you present your body as a living sacrifice for God's glory?
❑ Yes ❑ No If so, tell Him so in a prayer right now.

LEARNING THE DISCIPLE'S PERSONALITY

Read the section "Who Are You?" (p. 138) in the Disciple's Personality presentation.

Answer the following questions.

- **Are you a natural person whose spirit is dead? Do your bodily senses and your natural desires control you?**
  ❑ Yes ❑ No
- **Are you a worldly Christian who has allowed Christ to enter your life but is still being mastered by the desires of the flesh? Is the big *I* still in control? ❑ Yes ❑ No**
- **Are you a spiritual Christian who has been crucified with Christ and is being controlled by the Holy Spirit?**
  ❑ Yes ❑ No

Read 1 Thessalonians 5:23-24 in the margin. What do these verses tell you about the support you have for living blamelessly?
❑ Living a holy life is too difficult; it's all up to me, and I can't handle it.
❑ The Lord Jesus Christ who calls me will empower me to use my body, soul, and spirit in right living.

"May God himself, the God of peace, sanctify you through and through. May your whole spirit, soul and body be kept blameless at the coming of our Lord Jesus Christ. The one who calls you is faithful and he will do it" (1 Thess. 5:23-24).

These verses assure you that the Lord who calls you to serve Him will be faithful to help you act in the right way. He has sent the Holy Spirit to help you in this daily challenge.

On the next page is the spiritual-Christian illustration with blanks for you to add the Scripture references that go with it, as you learned yesterday. Many of these are memory verses you have learned in this study. Say them aloud as you write the references on the illustration. Refer to the Disciple's Personality

presentation (pp. 133–39) if you need help. By the end of this study you should be able to draw the complete Disciple's Personality and to explain it in your own words.

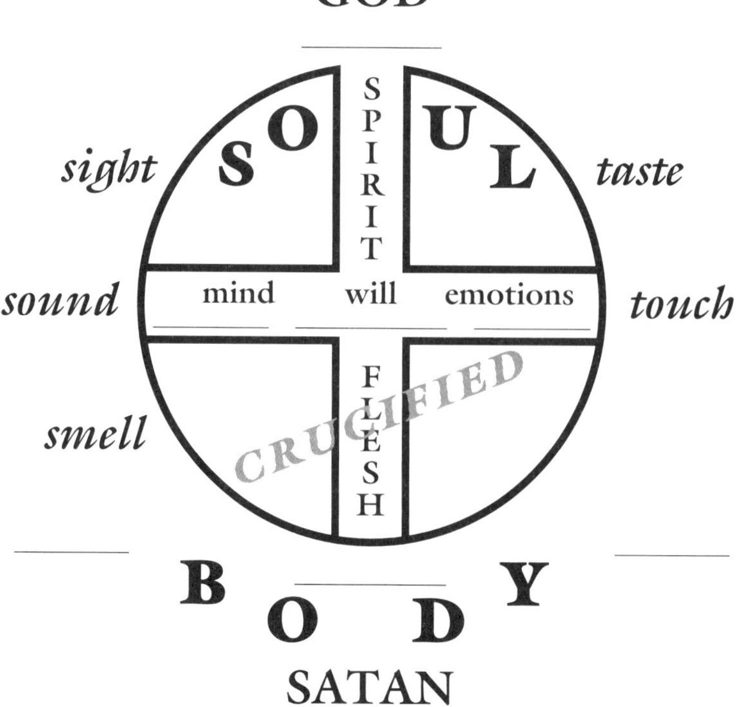

The Disciple's Personality presentation has been used many times to win someone to faith in Christ. David Carter, while serving as a Florida pastor, was visiting a couple he had visited several times before. The wife was a Christian, but the husband, an unbeliever, had always been unwilling to listen to a traditional gospel presentation. This time David decided to use the Disciple's Personality to confront the man with his spiritual condition. Drawing the natural-person and spiritual-Christian diagrams, he asked the man, "Which are you?" The husband pointed to the natural person. David asked, "Which would you like to be?" He pointed to the spiritual-Christian diagram and replied, "I've always wanted to be a Christian." David then led the man to pray to receive Christ as Savior and Lord.

"I've always wanted to be a Christian."

After the prayer the wife spoke up: "I am not either one." David replied, "I may have a diagram that represents you." When he drew the worldly-Christian diagram, she immediately said, "That's me!" David then led her to rededicate her life to Christ.

After learning the Disciple's Personality, you will be able to use it not only to lead persons to salvation but also to help others—

- deal with their emotions;

- close the door to Satan;
- renew their minds;
- find assurance that they can say no to temptation.

IN THE CARPENTER'S SHOP

Review your work this week and recall your efforts to get rid of the old self and to put on new actions and thoughts. How has the Holy Spirit helped you become more Christlike? Answer these questions about the area of change you identified on page 76:

Something I have been getting rid of this week:

____

Something Christ has been adding to my character this week:

____

Stop and pray. Thank God for helping you in the ways you listed. Ask Him to continue giving you the courage to make changes.

In your quiet time today read Philippians 1:19-26, which describes the priority Paul placed on exalting Christ in his body. Then complete the Daily Master Communication Guide in the margin.

HAS THIS WEEK MADE A DIFFERENCE?

Review "My Walk with the Master This Week" at the beginning of this week's material. Mark the activities you have finished by drawing vertical lines in the diamonds beside them. Finish any incomplete activities. Think about what you will say during your group session about your work on these activities.

As you complete your study of "Present Your Body," I hope that you have gained new insights about why you sometimes take actions that contradict your good intentions. I hope that you have committed each part of your body to the Lord's service and that you will let the Holy Spirit help you when you are tempted to make wrong choices.

DAILY MASTER COMMUNICATION GUIDE

PHILIPPIANS 1:19-26

What God said to me:

____

____

____

____

____

____

____

____

What I said to God:

____

____

____

____

____

____

____

____

____

WEEK 5

Be Filled with the Spirit

This Week's Goal

You will be able to allow the Holy Spirit to fill you.

My Walk with the Master This Week

You will complete the following activities to develop the six biblical disciplines. When you have completed each activity, draw a vertical line in the diamond beside it.

SPEND TIME WITH THE MASTER

◇ Have a quiet time each day, working toward the goal of having quiet times 21 consecutive days. Write the number of minutes you spend in your quiet time each day: Sunday:___ Monday:___ Tuesday:___ Wednesday:___ Thursday:___ Friday:___ Saturday:___

LIVE IN THE WORD

◇ Read your Bible every day. Write what God says to you and what you say to God.

◇ Memorize Ephesians 5:18.

◇ Review Philippians 2:13, Romans 12:1-2, Galatians 5:22-23, and 1 Corinthians 6:19-20.

◇ Using the Hearing the Word form, write notes from a sermon or a Bible study to apply in your life this week.

PRAY IN FAITH

◇ Pray for persons in your circles of influence.

FELLOWSHIP WITH BELIEVERS

◇ Share with another church member what God is doing in your life—struggles as well as victories.

WITNESS TO THE WORLD

◇ Write your testimony, using the ideas in "How to Write Your Testimony." Be ready to share it at the next group session.

MINISTER TO OTHERS

◇ Explain how to apply the Disciple's Personality, using James 4:1-8.

This Week's Scripture-Memory Verse

"Do not get drunk on wine, which leads to debauchery. Instead, be filled with the Spirit" (Eph. 5:18).

DAY 1

A Changed Life

When I was a freshman in college, the Holy Spirit created in my heart an overwhelming desire to bear witness to Christ. In the months that followed, His presence overcame my natural shyness and thrust me several times each week into the streets and bars to witness. However, I was not successful in leading persons to Christ. I memorized Scriptures, studied soul-winning books, and prayed. But something was missing.

One day I received a booklet that told about the experiences of D. L. Moody, R. A. Torrey, Billy Sunday, Billy Graham, and others whose ministries had been transformed when they experienced the filling of the Holy Spirit. I had a burning desire to be used by God, but no one could tell me how. Finally, a friend lent me the book *The Holy Spirit: Who He Is and What He Does* by R. A. Torrey. For the first time I realized that the Holy Spirit is a person who possesses us instead of a power, an influence, or an attitude we possess. I learned that the Holy Spirit, who lives in me, wants to fill me for service. By the next evening I had finished the book and was ready to follow its instructions to be filled with the Spirit. I confessed all of my sins, presented myself fully to God, and asked in faith for the Holy Spirit to fill me. As I confessed my sins, I realized how much the Holy Spirit loved me and had been grieved by my ignoring Him. Then I presented my body, will, emotions, mind, and spirit to be used by God in any way. I accepted by faith the filling of the Holy Spirit without an outward sign or manifestation. I told God, "I will accept the fact that I am filled with the Spirit on the basis of faith in the Word, no matter what happens afterward." I immediately sensed a deep awareness of the Spirit's love, which has grown stronger through the years as my relationship with God has deepened.

The Holy Spirit is a person who possesses us instead of a power, an influence, or an attitude we possess.

The next morning when I went to class, I was so aware of the Spirit's presence that I wanted to move over on the sidewalk to let Him walk beside me. That evening I witnessed to a boy on the street, and he accepted Christ as his Savior. Two nights later, two teenagers accepted Christ. The following night a man professed faith in Christ; the night after, another man did.

I remarked to a friend: "I don't see how this can continue. Every night I go out to witness, someone accepts Christ." That night no one did. I asked forgiveness for daring to think I had won those persons to Christ myself. God refilled me with His Spirit when I was willing to confess my sin, yield myself to Him, and ask in faith. Once again the persons to whom I witnessed accepted Christ.

In the years since that experience the Holy Spirit has taught me that the secret is to be filled for each task of service. Thousands of times

DAILY MASTER COMMUNICATION GUIDE

ACTS 2:1-21

What God said to me:

____

____

____

____

____

____

____

____

What I said to God:

____

____

____

____

____

____

____

____

when I have sinned, I have asked Him to refill me, and He has done so. The filling of the Spirit energizes and empowers different gifts in different persons, but in every case the result brings glory to Christ and attracts others to Him.

In the previous account what was the turning point at which God was able to do as He desired in my life?

____

The turning point in my story was when I asked in faith for the Holy Spirit to fill me after I had confessed my sins and had yielded myself to God. Until that point I had not allowed Him to work through me in His fullness.

Every person who has been born of the Spirit has the Holy Spirit living in his or her heart. Romans 8:16 says, "The Spirit himself testifies with our spirit that we are God's children." However, not everyone is filled with the Spirit and equipped for service (see Rom. 8:9).

Look again at Romans 8:16. Do you have the Holy Spirit living in you? ❑ Yes ❑ No ❑ Not sure

If you have given your life to Christ, He lives in you through His Spirit. However, you may or may not be filled with the Spirit at the present time.

Read Ephesians 5:18: "Do not get drunk on wine, which leads to debauchery. Instead, be filled with the Spirit."

Are you filled with the Spirit right now? ❑ Yes ❑ No ❑ Not sure

God wants your personality to be filled and overflowing with His Spirit. As you yield yourself to God, He takes control of every facet of your personality. Your inner self is integrated, and you experience constant fellowship with Him.

The purpose of this week's study is to explain God's purpose in filling you with the Spirit and to show you how to be filled daily. As a result of this week's study, you should be able to—

- explain the relationship between God's Spirit and the human spirit;
- list four important facts about being filled with the Holy Spirit;
- identify two purposes of being filled and explain the way God accomplishes each purpose;
- list three steps to being filled with the Spirit.

WHAT IT MEANS TO BE FILLED

A distinct difference exists between having the Spirit of God in you and being filled with the Spirit. Peter is a good example of this difference.

Even before Pentecost Peter had the Spirit of Christ. John 20:22 says, "With that he [Christ] breathed on them and said, 'Receive the Holy Spirit.' " In this verse Jesus breathed the Spirit into the disciples. This allowed the disciples to take up His mission, which they could accomplish only under the Spirit's leadership. But even though Peter had the Spirit of Christ in him already, at Pentecost a major change occurred in his life. When the Holy Spirit came in His fullness on the church, Peter was filled with the Spirit.

Before Pentecost Peter was cowardly and denied Jesus. Hot-tempered, he cut off the ear of the high priest's servant with a sword. After Pentecost we see no evidence of instability or superficiality in Peter. He became a totally different person. He began to preach boldly, he allowed God to work miracles through him, he proclaimed Christ while he risked his life, and he spoke with certainty and faith.

EXPERIENCING THE SPIRIT'S POWER

Everyone who has accepted Christ has the Spirit of Christ living in him or her. Read 2 Corinthians 1:21-22 in the margin.

"It is God who makes both us and you stand firm in Christ. He anointed us, set his seal of ownership on us, and put his Spirit in our hearts as a deposit, guaranteeing what is to come" (2 Cor. 1:21-22).

But a distinct difference exists between having a small amount of water in a cup and having the water fill or overflow the cup. That is why Jesus spoke of the Spirit's overflowing you. Read John 7:38-39 in the margin.

" 'Whoever believes in me, as the Scripture has said, streams of living water will flow from within him.' By this he meant the Spirit, whom those who believed in him were later to receive" (John 7:38-39).

The Holy Spirit wants to flow through you like the living water Jesus mentioned. Whenever the disciples in the Book of Acts encountered persons who were not filled with the Spirit, they prayed for them to be filled. Then God would move in their lives.

Ephesians 5:18 is this week's Scripture-memory verse. Turn to page 92 and read it aloud to begin learning it.

Today's Christians face the same problem the disciples faced—trying to fight spiritual battles with human resources. A majority of Christians live and serve as if Pentecost never happened. They try to obey Christ's commands in their own strength; yet they wonder how Satan so often outsmarts and overpowers them. They ignore the mission of the Holy Spirit, who came to continue Jesus' roles of inspiring, empowering, and guiding them. For them, the third member of the Trinity—the Holy Spirit—is almost "the unknown God." They think of Him as an influence, an attitude, or a way to express the fact that God is everywhere.

Is the Holy Spirit a personal, intimate friend who fills your life?
❑ Yes ❑ No ❑ Not sure

You may have tried to witness or teach a Bible study without relying on the Holy Spirit's power. You may have tried to solve a problem in your personal life, such as dealing with a rebellious child or improving an estranged relationship, without asking God to fill you with His Spirit.

The solution to your inadequacy lies in experiencing the Holy Spirit's presence and power as the disciples did at Pentecost. Pentecost cannot be repeated any more than Calvary can be repeated. However, Christians can lay hold of the power of Pentecost just as surely as they can experience the redemption of Calvary. This week you will learn more about how this occurs.

IN THE CARPENTER'S SHOP

One work of the Holy Spirit is to help you be like Jesus. Today you will choose another area of your life in which you want to be more Christlike.

Read the Scriptures in the margin that relate to anger and similar behaviors. From the verses marked "The World's Way" identify a specific behavior you want to get rid of. From the verses marked "The Spirit's Way" identify an action you will take to replace it. I have given you an example. Each day this week you will record your progress in working on this behavior.

Here is an example.

Behavior I want to work on: becoming angry and saying things I later regret

An action I will take to put off the old self: ask the Holy Spirit to teach me how to let Him control me and my tongue even when something angers me

An action I will take to let the Holy Spirit make me more like Christ: be more loving and kind in all of my relationships

Now you try it.

Behavior I want to work on: More patience

An action I will take to put off the old self:

When I feel anxiety or frustation
Stop and Ask the Holy Spirit to help me

An action I will take to let the Holy Spirit make me more like Christ:

Study His word and get even more of it in my heart

Stop and pray that you will constantly be filled with the Spirit and that He will work through you.

The World's Way

"Now you must rid yourselves of all such things as these: anger, rage, malice, slander, and filthy language from your lips" (Col. 3:8).

"The acts of the sinful nature are obvious: sexual immorality, impurity and debauchery. … I warn you, as I did before, that those who live like this will not inherit the kingdom of God" (Gal. 5:19-21).

"Get rid of all bitterness, rage and anger, brawling and slander, along with every form of malice" (Eph. 4:31).

The Spirit's Way

"As God's chosen people, holy and dearly loved, clothe yourselves with compassion, kindness, humility, gentleness and patience" (Col. 3:12).

"The fruit of the Spirit is love, joy, peace, patience, kindness, goodness, faithfulness, gentleness and self-control" (Gal. 5: 22-23).

"Be kind and compassionate to one another, forgiving each other, just as in Christ God forgave you" (Eph. 4:32).

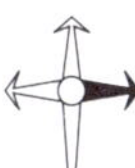

Share with a fellow church member your struggles and victories. Share with that person the area of your life you selected for the Holy Spirit to help you change.

Read Acts 2:1-21, the passage about the day of Pentecost, during your quiet time today. Then complete the Daily Master Communication Guide on page 94.

DAY 2

Your Spirit and God's Spirit

When you are born of the Spirit, your spirit is made alive, and you are able to respond spiritually. The Holy Spirit helps you—
- understand spiritual things;
- allow God to work through you.

"The man without the Spirit does not accept the things that come from the Spirit of God, for they are foolishness to him, and he cannot understand them, because they are spiritually discerned" (1 Cor. 2:14).

SPIRITUAL UNDERSTANDING

Read 1 Corinthians 2:14 in the margin. What can people understand without the Spirit's help? Check the correct answer.

❑ The deep things of God
❑ The basic truths of God
❑ No spiritual truths

Without the Spirit a person can understand nothing about God.

Read John 16:8-11 in the margin. In the blanks write ways the Holy Spirit convicts the world.

" 'When he comes, he will convict the world of guilt in regard to sin and righteousness and judgment: in regard to sin, because men do not believe in me; in regard to righteousness, because I am going to the Father, where you can see me no longer; and in regard to judgment, because the prince of this world now stands condemned' " (John 16:8-11).

The Holy Spirit convicts people of ______________ because they do not believe in Jesus.

The Holy Spirit convicts the world of ________________________ by His sinless life.

The Holy Spirit convicts the world in ________________ by condemning and judging Satan. Anyone who follows Satan, therefore, is also condemned.

The answers are *sin, unrighteousness,* and *judgment.*

The Holy Spirit helps you understand the truths of God. Read 1 Corinthians 2:9-10 in the margin. I have heard this verse applied to what is in heaven, but it clearly says that God, through His Spirit, has already revealed truths that were not previously known by humankind.

"It is written:
'No eye has seen,
no ear has heard,
no mind has conceived
what God has prepared for
those who love him'
but God has revealed it to us by his Spirit" (1 Cor. 2:9-10).

Read 1 Corinthians 2:12 and John 14:26 in the margin. What is the Spirit trying to teach you?

"We have not received the spirit of the world but the Spirit who is from God, that we may understand what God has freely given us" (1 Cor. 2:12).

" 'The counselor, the Holy Spirit, whom the Father will send in my name, will teach you all things and will remind you of everything I have said to you' " (John 14:26).

The Holy Spirit helps you recall Christ's teachings. He will teach you all things (see John 16:15) and guide you into His truth.

THE SPIRIT WORKS THROUGH YOU

Not only does the Holy Spirit make you aware of the truth, but He also does God's work through you and other believers.

Read Acts 1:8 in the margin. What does the Spirit enable you to do?

"You will receive power when the Holy Spirit comes on you; and you will be my witnesses in Jerusalem, and in all Judea and Samaria, and to the ends of the earth" (Acts 1:8).

The Holy Spirit enables you to be Christ's witness. Zechariah 4:6 says, "Not by might nor by power, but my spirit, says the Lord Almighty."

Read Acts 4:8 and Acts 4:31 in the margin and underline the words showing that the filling of the Spirit was the key element in God's speaking or working through persons.

"Peter, filled with the Holy Spirit, said to them: 'Rulers and elders of the people! If we are being called to account today for an act of kindness shown to a cripple and are asked how he was healed, then know this, you and all the people of Israel: It is by the name of Jesus Christ of Nazareth, whom you crucified but whom God raised from the dead, that this man stands before you healed' " (Acts 4:8).

"After they prayed, the place where they were meeting was shaken. And they were all filled with the Holy Spirit and spoke the word of God boldly" (Acts 4:31).

Perhaps you underlined such words as "Peter, filled with the Holy Spirit, said to them" in the first verse and "they were all filled with the Holy Spirit and spoke" in the second verse.

Review by listing the two things the Spirit enables you to do. Check your answers by looking at the list on page 97.

1.

2.

LETTING THE SPIRIT ENTER

The Spirit of God and the human spirit are different. God is divine; you are human. God's Spirit enters your personality through your human spirit. You are responsible for letting the Spirit of God come in or for shutting Him out.

Read Revelation 3:20: " 'Here I am! I stand at the door and knock. If anyone hears my voice and opens the door, I will come in and eat with him, and he with me.' " How does this verse picture Jesus?

This verse depicts Jesus standing outside the door of your heart and gently asking for entrance. People who accept Christ open their lives to Him and invite Him to dwell in them. When you open the door to His marvelous invitation, God's Spirit enters your life and brings peace to your soul.

Pray for persons within your circles of influence—those with whom you associate occasionally or regularly. Pray that you will have opportunities to share God's love and His availability to them. Write their names on your Prayer-Covenant List (p. 143).

A CONTINUAL FILLING

A true disciple lets the Spirit of God continually fill and control his or her entire personality, as this week's Scripture-memory verse instructs.

Stop and say aloud your memory verse, Ephesians 5:18.

Read Acts 4:29: " 'Now, Lord, consider their threats and enable your servants to speak your word with great boldness.' " What did the apostles ask for when they were threatened?

To be able to speak

When they were threatened, the apostles did not ask for release or safety. They asked to be able to speak the Word with great boldness, and God gave them boldness. As a result, many people came to Christ.

Ask the Holy Spirit to fill you this week and to give you boldness to speak for Christ.

IN THE CARPENTER'S SHOP

How is the Holy Spirit working to change you into the image of Christ? What progress are you making in developing Christlike character?

In day 1 you listed a behavior related to anger that you hoped to get rid of to be more like Jesus. Today describe an instance in which you have already worked to set aside that behavior.

the consistent strange attitude

from my husband and not allowing

DAILY MASTER COMMUNICATION GUIDE

ACTS 4:13-31

What God said to me:

What I said to God:

Read Acts 4:13-31, the passage from which the verse you read about boldness is taken, during your quiet time today. Then complete the Daily Master Communication Guide on page 99.

DAY 3

Filled Without Limit

In day 2 you learned that true disciples let the Spirit of God continually fill and control their entire personalities. However, not all Christians allow God to control their lives. Worldly Christians still struggle with the big *I* of the natural person.

Based on what you learned as you studied the Disciple's Personality, describe in your own words why the Spirit of God does not fill everyone's personality.

they have not asked.
____

____

You may have answered something like this: Not everyone has opened the door of his or her spirit to God's Spirit. You must first open the door before the Spirit of God can fill your personality.

CONTROLLED BY THE SPIRIT

You have the Spirit of Christ dwelling in you if you belong to Jesus. You may treat Him as a guest, a servant, a tenant, or Lord and Master—the owner of the property. But the Spirit will not fill you completely until you acknowledge Christ's lordship and submit to His personal and divine authority. First Thessalonians 5:23, in the margin, describes what God does in your personality.

"May God himself, the God of peace, sanctify you through and through. May your whole spirit, soul and body be kept blameless at the coming of our Lord Jesus Christ" (1 Thess. 5:23).

***Sanctify* means *to set apart* or *to cleanse.* Write *T* beside the statement that best expresses the truth of 1 Thessalonians 5:23.**
T **God sets apart or cleanses your entire personality.**
___ **God cleanses your spirit only.**

Your entire personality is cleansed as God's Spirit controls your spirit. When God sanctifies your entire personality, He and you enjoy mutual fellowship.

Although you have the Holy Spirit living in you, you might not be

giving Him His rightful place. Check the box that best describes how the Holy Spirit would say that you treat Him.

- ☑ As a guest
- ☐ As a servant
- ☐ As a tenant
- ☑ As Master—the owner of the property

What relationship should exist between God's Spirit and your spirit? Check the correct answer.

- ☐ Your spirit should control God's Spirit.
- ☐ God's Spirit and your spirit should be on equal terms.
- ☑ God's Spirit should control your spirit.

God's will is that you be completely controlled by His Spirit. This week's Scripture-memory verse, Ephesians 5:18, tells how this occurs.

Say aloud this week's Scripture-memory verse, Ephesians 5:18, as you continue to memorize it.

OCCUPIED WITH CHRIST

John 3:34, in the margin, states that Jesus was filled with God's Spirit without limit. Jesus had the Spirit filling Him constantly and empowering Him in everything He did. I urge you to open your entire life to the Holy Spirit.

" 'The one whom God has sent speaks the words of God, for God gives the Spirit without limit' " (John 3:34).

What would be required for you to follow totally the Holy Spirit's guidance in everything you do? Check the following statements that apply.

I would have to—

- ☑ confess and forsake sin in my life;
- ☑ spend more time in Bible study to hear the Spirit speaking to me;
- ☑ spend more time in prayer asking for the Spirit to reveal God's will for me;
- ☑ ask the Spirit to fill me;
- ☑ turn to God first when a crisis occurs rather than as the last resort;
- ☑ be alert and open to opportunities to witness;
- ☑ seek the Christ-honoring solution to situations rather than my solutions;
- ☐ take this action: daily @ all times.

In his book *The Full Blessing of Pentecost* Andrew Murray lists seven main points about a Christian's being filled with the Holy Spirit.

As you read the following quotation by Andrew Murray, underline troublesome areas that limit your being filled with the Holy Spirit.

"Without being filled with the Spirit, it is utterly impossible that an individual Christian or a church can ever live or work as God desires." —Andrew Murray

> 1. *It is the will of God that every one of His children should live entirely and unceasingly under the control of the Holy Spirit.*
> 2. *Without being filled with the Spirit, it is utterly impossible that an individual Christian or a church can ever live or work as God desires.*
> 3. *Everywhere and in everything we see the proofs, in the life and experience of Christians, that this blessing is but little enjoyed in the Church, and alas! is but little sought for.*
> 4. *This blessing is prepared for us and God waits to bestow it. Our faith may expect it with the greatest confidence.*
> 5. *The great hindrance in the way is that the self-life, and the world, which it uses for its own service and pleasure, usurp the place that Christ ought to occupy.*
> 6. *We cannot be filled with the Spirit until we are prepared to yield ourselves to be led by the Lord Jesus to forsake and sacrifice every thing for this pearl of great price.*[1]

Now read the following quotation by L. L. Letgers. As you read, think about ways your life resembles or does not resemble this description.

> *Your evidence that you are filled with the spirit is that Jesus becomes everything to you. You see Him. You are occupied with Him. You are fully satisfied with Jesus. He becomes real, and when you witness about Him, the Holy Spirit witnesses with you regarding the truth about Him. … Jesus is your Lord and Master and you rest in His Lordship. … The real evidence of a Spirit-filled life is … first, that others see the Holy Spirit working in your life the character of Christ, the fruit of the Spirit, and second, that you in your own private life see in the Book the things of Jesus, and that you are personally rejoicing in Him, and are occupied with Him.*[2]

Which of the following best reflect your response to the quotations you read about being filled with the Spirit? Check all that apply.

❑ I have never known the kind of life described.
❑ Lord, I have wandered from You. I want to return.
❑ I have not yet arrived, but I'm working on living in this manner.
❑ Lord, please fill me so that I may experience this kind of life.
❑ Lord God, I praise You for the mighty work You have done in my life.
❑ Other: ______________________________

One aid to being occupied with Jesus is to apply the word you hear preached. Genuinely looking forward to the times you hear God's word preached can help you discern its relevance for you and can make you receptive to the Holy Spirit as He speaks to you through it. The next activity will help you look for the Holy Spirit's work in your life.

Write notes from a sermon or a Bible study—something you learned or want to learn more about—on the Hearing the Word form on page 141.

Read Luke 24:13-53, the passage that describes Jesus' ascension into heaven, during your quiet time today. See how God speaks to you through this passage. Then complete the Daily Master Communication Guide in the margin.

DAY 4

How to Be Filled

If you still have questions about how to be filled with the Holy Spirit, this week's Scripture-memory verse contains several clues about how this occurs. It gives four important facts about the directive "Be filled with the Spirit."

Before you read about these important facts, say aloud this week's Scripture-memory verse, Ephesians 5:18, three times from memory. Also take this opportunity to review the other verses you have memorized since you began this study.

We can learn a great deal by examining the meaning of this verse in its original language. The phrase *be filled* is—

- passive voice. *Passive* means that you cannot do something yourself. Someone has to do it to you. Only God can fill you. You cannot do it to yourself or cause yourself to be filled.
- present tense. You are to be filled now. This refers to the state you are to be in.
- continuous action. Present tense in Greek indicates continuous action. It means *keep on being filled*. Although your conversion was a one-time experience, the filling of the Spirit is not. It needs to keep on happening. Envision a pipe through which water passes at all times. If the Spirit is filling you, He is always going through you as He works to minister to others.
- imperative mood. "Be filled" is an order, a command to all Christians. It is not just an option or something you can dismiss because you do not understand it. It is a teaching of God's Word. My understanding of being filled was greatly affected by my personal experience of being filled with the Holy Spirit, which I related in day 1. However, the Bible teaches that some Christians are filled when they are saved, like Cornelius in Acts 10.

DAILY MASTER COMMUNICATION GUIDE

LUKE 24:13-53

What God said to me:

____

____

____

____

____

____

____

What I said to God:

____

____

____

____

____

____

____

____

Go back and draw a star beside the fact you most need to be reminded of. Why do you need this reminder?

Because we tend to forget sometimes
this is the main reason why there are worldly Christians

THE SPIRIT FLOWS THROUGH YOU

How can someone personally experience the filling of the Holy Spirit? If you belong to Jesus, His Spirit already dwells in you. But His purpose is to fill you continually and to flow through you to others. You are not to be a container but a conduit or a channel for Him. The filling of the Spirit enables God to communicate His message to others through you.

A Christian must take three steps to be filled and controlled by the Holy Spirit:

"If we confess our sins, he is faithful and just and will forgive us our sins and purify us from all unrighteousness" (1 John 1:9).

" 'If you then, though you are evil, know how to give good gifts to your children, how much more will your Father in heaven give the Holy Spirit to those who ask him!' " (Luke 11:13).

1. Confess your sin, disobedience, emptiness, and need for God's cleansing. Read 1 John 1:9 in the margin.
2. Present every member of your body to be made a righteous instrument in God's hands. Recall Romans 12:1, one of your Scripture-memory verses.
3. Ask God to fill, control, and empower you, as Luke 11:13, in the margin, promises. Believe that God has answered your prayer.

What steps do you need to take to experience the filling of God's Spirit? Bow your head now and open your spirit to the Spirit of God. Follow the three steps listed above. Write what you experienced by faith.

A calmness, sense of true peace.

Stop and pray. Say aloud Ephesians 5:18, this week's Scripture-memory verse. Thank God for the gift of His fullness.

"Speak to one another with psalms, hymns and spiritual songs. Sing and make music in your heart to the Lord" (Eph. 5:19).

"Always giving thanks to God the Father for everything, in the name of our Lord Jesus Christ" (Eph. 5:20).

In the verses in the margin find two results of being filled with the Spirit.

1. Ephesians 5:19: Speaking to one another through spiritual things

2. Ephesians 5:20: Always giving thanks

Christians today can be like those in the early church, in which Spirit-filled members learned to worship God with thanksgiving for everything. These early Christians often expressed thanksgiving through music. You may have responded like this: 1. speaking to one another and singing to the Lord, 2. giving thanks.

GOD'S PURPOSES IN FILLING YOU

God has a double purpose in filling you with His Spirit. First, God wants to develop Christlike character in you. In 1 Thessalonians 5:23 Paul prayed that your personality would be found blameless: "May God himself, the God of peace, sanctify you through and through. May your whole spirit, soul and body be kept blameless at the coming of our Lord Jesus Christ." Second, God wants to empower you to do His work.

" 'You will receive power when the Holy Spirit comes on you; and you will be my witnesses in Jerusalem, and in all Judea and Samaria, and to the ends of the earth' " (Acts 1:8).

"After they prayed, the place where they were meeting was shaken. And they were all filled with the Holy Spirit and spoke the word of God boldly" (Acts 4:31).

Read Acts 1:8 and Acts 4:31 in the margin. Explain what the Holy Spirit enables you to do.

Be a witness. Speak the word Boldly

The Holy Spirit provided power for witnessing with boldness. The disciples, timid and fearful earlier, now preached fearlessly. The Holy Spirit empowers ordinary people to testify boldly even under difficult circumstances. You need the power of the Spirit to enable you to witness. Being bold does not mean that you are never nervous or that you never fear an opportunity to witness. It means that you have the courage to do it even when you are afraid.

Being bold does not mean that you are never nervous or that you never fear an opportunity to witness. It means that you have the courage to do it even when you are afraid.

I hope that you also look forward to the time when you can share your prepared testimony with persons in your circles of influence.

APPLYING THE DISCIPLE'S PERSONALITY

Each week of this study you have learned a different component of the Disciple's Personality. Now that you have learned the entire presentation, you may wonder how you can use this knowledge in everyday situations.

The Disciple's Personality contains many Bible truths that apply to a variety of situations:

1. Use it to evaluate your spiritual growth.
2. Apply its teachings to gain victory in your personal life:
   a. Use it when you face temptation to overcome the flesh and Satan.
   b. Use it in prayer as you dedicate your total personality to the Master. Pray about each part of your personality.
   c. Use it to review the Scripture-memory verses related to the victorious life.
   d. Use it to review Bible teachings about each part of your personality.
3. Draw it to help others evaluate whether they are natural, worldly, or spiritual persons and to explain how they can apply it to their lives.
4. Use it with an unsaved person to explain how to become a disciple of Christ. First draw and explain the Natural Person. Next draw and explain the Spiritual Christian. If the person accepts Christ, draw the Worldly Christian to show how not to live. If he or she does not accept Christ, you may need to draw and explain the Worldly Chris-

tian to explain why some Christians do not live victorious lives. Otherwise, do not present the Worldly Christian to this person.

Practice explaining in your own words how to apply the Disciple's Personality, using the basic drawing below. Your leader showed you in the previous group session how to apply the illustration, using James 4:1-8. Close the door of the flesh as you draw a cross in the center of the circle to encompass *spirit, flesh, mind, will,* and *emotions.* Write *crucified* across *flesh.* Now write *submit* above the circle. Write *Draw near to God* and draw an arrow toward God. Write *God will draw near to you* and draw an arrow from *God* toward the circle. Write *resist* below the circle and draw an arrow toward *Satan.* Write *will flee from you* below *Satan* and draw a downward arrow. See page 140 if you need help with your drawing.

GOD

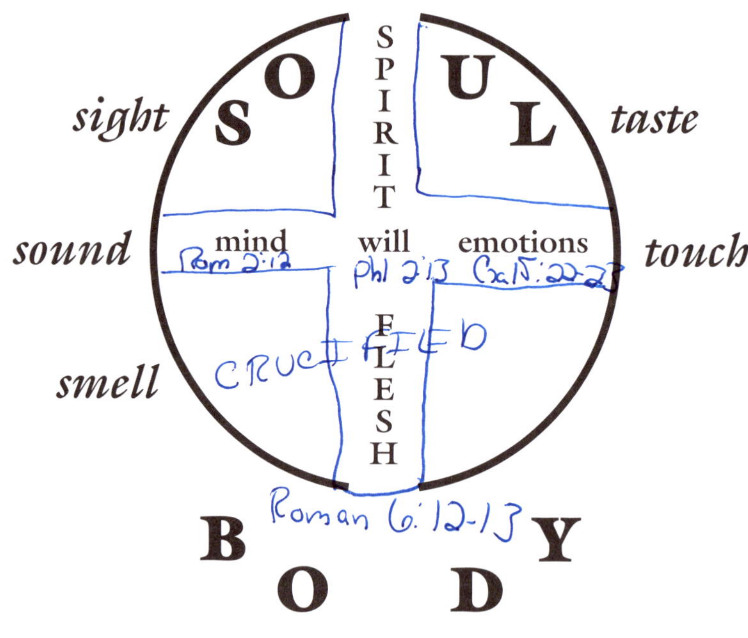

SATAN

Now use James 4:1-8 to explain the presentation in your own words.

Be about God's business at all times
Pray to get revelation from Him of what I need if He tells me what I need, I will have it, walk in obidience and He will give me my desires.

Have you already used the Disciple's Personality? ☑ Yes ❑ No If so, describe your experience below. If not, be open to ways the Holy Spirit reveals to you.

Just only in words not visual the person received what I said.

IN THE CARPENTER'S SHOP
How is the Holy Spirit guiding your efforts to put off the old self and to replace it with the new?

In day 2 you recorded your progress in tearing down old habits related to anger. Today describe what you see Christ adding to your life to replace that old trait or behavior.

Patience and allowing me to have a more reverance time with Him

During your quiet time today read Acts 10, describing Cornelius's salvation and the filling of the Holy Spirit. Let God speak to you through this passage. Then complete the Daily Master Communication Guide in the margin.

DAILY MASTER COMMUNICATION GUIDE

ACTS 10

What God said to me:

What I said to God:

DAY 5

Accomplishing God's Purposes

You learned in day 4 that God wants to accomplish two purposes in the life of a Spirit-filled Christian:

- To develop Christlike character
- To equip you for ministry

"For this very reason, make every effort to add to your faith goodness; and to goodness, knowledge; and to knowledge, self-control; and to self-control, perseverance; and to perseverance, godliness; and to godliness, brotherly kindness; and to brotherly kindness, love. For if you possess these qualities in increasing measure, they will keep you from being ineffective and unproductive in your knowledge of our Lord Jesus Christ" (2 Pet. 1:5-8).

DEVELOPING CHRISTLIKE CHARACTER

The first purpose, developing Christlike character, is achieved through the fruit of the Spirit and the second through the gifts of the Spirit.

Let's look at the way the fruit of the Spirit produces Christlike character.

Review the fruit of the Spirit in Galatians 5:22-23, your Scripture-memory verses in week 3. Then read 2 Peter 1:5-8 in the margin, in which Peter named the building blocks of Christian character. List these qualities.

Faith	Goodness
knowledge	Self-control
perseverance	godliness
brotherly kindness	love

Why did Peter say that you need these qualities?

To be effective & productive

Peter said you need these qualities so that you will be effective and productive in the Christian life. A person who has life in the Spirit bears fruit for Christ.

IN THE CARPENTER'S SHOP

How has the Holy Spirit worked in you this week to build Christlike character? Are you getting rid of the old self and adding new behaviors to your life?

Answer the questions about the area related to anger that you identified on page 96.

Something I have been getting rid of this week:

the sense of wanting to overcome.

Something Christ has been adding to my character this week:

Endurance, Perseverance

Stop and thank God for the Holy Spirit, who molds you into Christlikeness.

EQUIPPING FOR MINISTRY

The Holy Spirit accomplishes the second purpose, equipping you for ministry, by bestowing gifts of the Spirit. He empowers you to minister to others through the gifts He has given you. When you see persons who are filled with the Spirit, you immediately see that they want to minister. They want to let God work through them and to join God on His mission. Only the continual filling and refilling of the Spirit can produce this desire. Fruit produces character, and gifts produce effectiveness in ministry.

Some gifts of the Holy Spirit are listed in 1 Corinthians 12:7-11 and Romans 12:6-8, which are in the margin. Read the verses and write any gift(s) you believe the Holy Spirit has given you.

To what extent have you developed the gift(s) you have been given? Write the number(s) beside the gift(s) you listed above.
1. none 2. some 3. much

Stop and ask God to help you surrender your gifts to Him and to help you find ways to develop your gifts to their fullest.

Christlike character and effectiveness in ministry are possible only through the continual filling of the Spirit. Trying to achieve either by your own efforts is an exercise in futility. *MasterLife 4: The Disciple's Mission*, will define the ministry gifts and will help you discover the gifts the Spirit has given you. Develop your spiritual gifts so that you can minister as the Spirit desires.

To summarize what you have learned about God's purposes in filling you with the Spirit, fill in the blanks below.

God's first purpose: ____________________

How He accomplishes it: ____________________

God's second purpose: ____________________

How He accomplishes it: ____________________

HOW TO WRITE YOUR TESTIMONY

You can compile facts about your Christian life in a clear, concise testimony. Here are reasons to write your testimony.

- To clarify experiences in your mind
- To allow your leader to give feedback so that you can sharpen your testimony

"To each one the manifestation of the Spirit is given for the common good. To one there is given through the Spirit the message of wisdom, to another the message of knowledge by means of the same Spirit, to another faith by the same Spirit, to another gifts of healing by that one Spirit, to another miraculous powers, to another prophecy, to another distinguishing between spirits, to another speaking in different kinds of tongues, and to still another the interpretation of tongues. All these are the work of one and the same Spirit, and he gives them to each one, just as he determines" (1 Cor. 12: 7-11).

"We have different gifts, according to the grace given us. If a man's gift is prophesying, let him use it in proportion to his faith. If it is serving, let him serve; if it is teaching, let him teach; if it is encouraging, let him encourage; if it is contributing to the needs of others, let him give generously; if it is leadership, let him govern diligently; if it is showing mercy, let him do it cheerfully" (Rom. 12:6-8).

Write the way you talk.

- To develop a standard testimony to adapt to specific situations
- To master your testimony so that you are ready to use it anytime

Essential Preliminary Steps

1. Use the brief testimony you wrote in week 3 and the notes you made in week 4 as resources for your first draft. After the first draft has been evaluated, you may rewrite it in a more polished version. Write the way you talk. Use *I* and *me*. Do not worry about formal rules of grammar. You will communicate your testimony verbally by sharing, not preaching.
2. Choose one of the following approaches to write the testimony.
   a. *Chronological*. This approach is better when enough significant experiences happened before your conversion to distinguish clearly between your life before and after conversion.

CHRONOLOGICAL

1. Before I met Christ
2. How I realized my need
3. How I became a Christian
4. What being a Christian means to me

   b. *Thematic*. This approach is the better choice when you were saved as a child and/or do not remember enough significant events before your conversion that the other person can identify with. Begin by focusing on an experience, problem, issue, or feeling, such as a fear of death, a desire for success, a basic character flaw, a search for identity, or a crisis.

THEMATIC

1. A theme, a need, or a problem
2. How I became a Christian
3. What being a Christian means to me

Begin with a brief testimony about your current situation:

- I have discovered how not to worry.
- I have discovered a purpose for living.
- I have overcome loneliness.
- I have overcome my fear of death.
- I have learned how to integrate my life into a meaningful whole.
- I have found the secret to a happy life.

State the theme and tell how you solved your problem. This flashback technique can take the place of telling your experience before conversion. It is also effective if you cannot remember the exact sequence of events in your conversion experience. Many people have full assurance that they are saved, but they have trouble identifying the exact time of their conversion. If that is your case, be sure that you are saved now. If you have doubt, talk with your *MasterLife* leader or with another Christian who can help you find assurance of salvation. The date of your conversion is not as important as your personal relationship with Christ as Savior and Lord. The flashback technique allows you to give the facts without detailing when they happened. Even though you may not remember consciously thinking through each of the four facts of the gospel (sin, sin's penalty, Christ's payment, and receiving Christ) at conversion, you can mention them in the flashback approach, since you have become aware of them and believe them now.

Check the approach above that you intend to use.

Writing Your Testimony

1. Write an interesting introduction about your life and attitudes before following Christ. Help the person see you as an ordinary person. Give a few brief facts about your early life to set the scene. Use facts that the person can identify with or that help him or her see you as a normal person. Sound adult, not juvenile. For example, do not say, "My dad used to set me on his knee and talk to me." Say, "One day as my dad and I were talking, he said ..." Do not reminisce too much about details that would be unimportant to a stranger. Use concrete words and word pictures to describe the situation. Be brief.
2. Highlight the events that led to your salvation (how you realized your need). Summarize the events that led you to realize your need for Christ. Avoid using the name of your church, your specific age, or the date of conversion unless the person hearing your testimony has the same background. Keep these facts general to make it easier for others to identify with you. Do not use religious jargon or church words that might not be understood by persons with limited or different religious backgrounds.
3. Summarize the facts of salvation (how you became a Christian).
   a. *Chronological.* Tell how you became aware that sin involves living an "I-controlled" life. State how you felt when you realized the penalty of sin. Explain how you knew that Christ paid the penalty for your sin. Summarize how you received Christ. Be sure to emphasize repentance and faith in Christ as the way to salvation.
   b. *Thematic.* Even if you cannot remember each of the previous stages clearly, you can state your realization without referring

Summarize the events that led you to realize your need for Christ.

Close your testimony in a way that leads to further conversation about salvation.

to the time you realized each. However, state with confidence that you received Christ and are following Him as your Lord.

Sometimes a personal testimony is a good way to begin a witnessing encounter. If you use your testimony to introduce a presentation of the gospel, you may omit the next point and tell how to receive Christ through the gospel presentation.

4. Share the results of knowing Christ as Lord and Savior (what being a Christian means to you). Quickly summarize the difference Christ has made in your life. Give concrete examples.
   a. Mention the struggles of your continuing pilgrimage so that you do not give the impression that you think you are perfect. For example, "Being a Christian doesn't mean that I don't have problems, but now Christ helps me through them."
   b. Do not spend too much time on this point. Many Christians tend to focus on what has happened since conversion. Mention it, but the non-Christian also needs to know how you reached this point. He should relate more to the beginning experience than to later experiences. Revise your testimony to focus on salvation.
5. Close your testimony in a way that leads to further conversation about salvation. Use questions such as:
   a. Has anything like that ever happened to you?
   b. Does that make sense to you?
   c. Have you ever thought that you would like to have such peace (assurance, joy, experience, and so on)?
   d. Do you know for certain that you have eternal life and that you will go to heaven when you die?

Evaluating Your Testimony

1. Check your testimony by using the following criteria. Revise your rough draft as needed. You will rewrite your testimony after it has been evaluated during your next group session.
   a. Does it have a clear story line that ties everything together?
   b. Are all four parts of the testimony developed proportionally?
   c. In explaining how you became a Christian, did you include the four doctrinal truths of the gospel (see p. 80)?
   d. Is the testimony too brief? Too long? Does it need details?
   e. Does the testimony conclude with a final sentence that will lead to further conversation?
   f. Does the testimony sound conversational, formal, or preachy?
2. Writing your testimony may be difficult. The time required to write it will depend on its complexity and on the number of times you have given it before. It does not relate to your intelligence or to your testimony's validity. Thinking about unpleasant events in your life may be upsetting. You may discover the need to be sure that you have been saved. Satan does not want you to prepare a testimony. Ask God to help you.

As you read this section, if you had any question about whether you are saved, you can receive Jesus Christ now by invitation. Romans 10:13 says, "Everyone who calls on the name of the Lord will be saved." You may use this prayer to express your commitment:

Lord Jesus, I am a sinner. I need You. I want You to be my Savior and Lord. I accept Your death on the cross as the payment for my sins, and I now entrust my life to Your care. Thank You for forgiving me and for giving me a new life. Please help me grow in my understanding of Your love and power so that my life will bring glory and honor to You. Amen.

Signed  Date ________

Write your testimony, using the ideas in "How to Write Your Testimony." Be ready to share it at the next group session. It should be only three minutes long. That is equivalent to about one page, typed and double-spaced, or two pages handwritten.

During your quiet time today read Romans 12:1-8, which mentions spiritual gifts that build up the body of Christ. Then complete the Daily Master Communication Guide in the margin.

HAS THIS WEEK MADE A DIFFERENCE?

Review "My Walk with the Master This Week" at the beginning of this week's material. Mark the activities you have finished by drawing vertical lines in the diamonds beside them. Finish any incomplete activities. Think about what you will say during your group session about your work on these activities.

As you complete your study of "Be Filled with the Spirit," consider the following statements and check the boxes beside those that apply.

- [x] **I am more aware than ever of the gracious gift of the Holy Spirit, who lives in me.**
- [x] **I desire to be filled with the Spirit and will take steps to be filled.**
- [x] **The filling of the Holy Spirit in me is already motivating me to use my gifts to minister to others.**
- [x] **The Holy Spirit has helped me build more Christlike character this week by tearing down old thoughts and actions and by replacing them with new ones.**

[1]Andrew Murray, *The Full Blessing of Pentecost* (Port Washington, Pa.: Christian Literature Crusade, 1954), 7.
[2]L. L. Letgers, *The Simplicity of the Spirit-Filled Life* (Farmingdale, N.Y.: Christian Witness, 1968), 51–52.

DAILY MASTER COMMUNICATION GUIDE

ROMANS 12:1-8

What God said to me:

What I said to God:

WEEK 6

Live Victoriously

This Week's Goal

You will be able to explain how you became a Christian and how to live a life of victory in the Spirit.

My Walk with the Master This Week

You will complete the following activities to develop the six biblical disciplines. When you complete each activity, draw a vertical line in the diamond beside it.

SPEND TIME WITH THE MASTER

◇ Have a quiet time each day. Write the number of minutes you spend in your quiet time each day: Sunday:___ Monday:___ Tuesday:___ Wednesday:___ Thursday:___ Friday:___ Saturday:___

LIVE IN THE WORD

◇ Read your Bible every day. Write what God says to you and what you say to God.

◇ Memorize Romans 6:12-13.

◇ Review Ephesians 5:18, Philippians 2:13, Romans 12:1-2, Galatians 5:22-23, and 1 Corinthians 6:19-20.

◇ Use the Hearing the Word form with a Sunday School lesson or a sermon.

PRAY IN FAITH

◇ Pray for two lost coworkers or neighbors.

FELLOWSHIP WITH BELIEVERS

◇ Share with your prayer partner ways the Holy Spirit helps you.

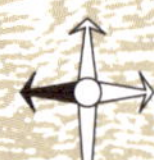

WITNESS TO THE WORLD

◇ Work on your testimony, using the ideas your leader gave you last week.

MINISTER TO OTHERS

◇ Practice giving your testimony.

◇ Draw and explain the Disciple's Personality.

◇ Explain how to apply the Disciple's Personality, using Galatians 5:16-25.

This Week's Scripture-Memory Verses

"Do not let sin reign in your mortal body so that you obey its evil desires. Do not offer the parts of your body to sin, as instruments of wickedness, but rather offer yourselves to God, as those who have been brought from death to life; and offer the parts of your body to him as instruments of righteousness" (Rom. 6:12-13).

DAY 1

Victory over Sin

As a group of Colorado pastors finished *MasterLife* training, one of them received a call to visit a young woman who had just attempted suicide. As the pastor spoke with the patient, her nurse remained in the hospital room. In counseling the young woman, the pastor related the basic elements of the Disciple's Personality he had just learned at the training. He explained how all aspects of our personality work together, why we make the choices we do, and how Satan influences us to sin.

When the pastor had finished the visit and left the room, the nurse followed him outside. "That was the most helpful thing I've ever heard," the nurse said. "Please tell me more." The pastor further explained how to be saved, and the nurse made a profession of faith.

"The fruit of that pastor's sharing the Disciple's Personality was immediate," recalled Jimmy Crowe, who was conducting the training. "It helped the patient, but it helped the nurse even more."

By learning how your personality works, you can understand how to live a victorious life. Just understanding these concepts does not stop sin in the world. Satan is always at work, seeking to devour anyone he can. Knowledge is power, but the real power is the Holy Spirit. By learning how easily you can falter and how easily you can leave open the door of the flesh, you can stay on guard against thoughts and actions that are part of the old self and can put Christlike traits in their place.

"Everyone born of God overcomes the world. This is the victory that has overcome the world, even our faith. Who is it that overcomes the world? Only he who believes that Jesus is the Son of God" (1 John 5:4-5).

When Jesus died on the cross and rose from the grave, He won the victory over sin. He promised that His disciples would share in His victory (see 1 John 5:4-5 in the margin). A victorious Christian life is a Spirit-filled life.

You discovered in last week's work that being filled with God's Spirit is a daily process of crucifying the flesh and allowing the Spirit to have control. In this week's study you will learn how to participate in the victory over sin that Jesus has already won for you. As a result of this week's study, you should be able to—

- explain how the Disciple's Personality can be used to bring defeat or to achieve victory;
- express how Jesus has ensured victory for His disciples;
- evaluate the degree to which you are living in victory.

INTERNAL CONFLICT

In every person a civil war rages between the forces of Satan and the forces of God. Every person is made in God's image. He or she has God's moral law stamped into his or her being. Yet this person's fallen bodily senses and fleshly desires are in control. Read about this person's dilemma in Romans 7:19-24 in the margin.

"What I do is not the good I want to do; no, the evil I do not want to do—this I keep on doing. Now if I do what I do not want to do, it is no longer I who do it, but it is sin living in me that does it. So I find this law at work: When I want to do good, evil is right there with me. For in my inner being I delight in God's law; but I see another law at work in the members of my body, waging war against the law of my mind and making me a prisoner of the law of sin at work within my members. What a wretched man I am! Who will rescue me from this body of death?" (Rom. 7:19-24).

Daily Master Communication Guide

Ephesians 5

What God said to me:

What I said to God:

Think about the passage you just read and write a brief summary of what Paul described.

You may have written a response similar to this: I want to do good, but I cannot because of sin. I am captive to the law of sin.

The worldly Christian is in a constant state of tension. Because the door of the flesh is still open and because the big *I* is still in control, evil desires enter and work to crowd out the Holy Spirit.

Read what Paul said about the worldly mind in Romans 8:6-8: "The mind of sinful man is death, but the mind controlled by the Spirit is life and peace; the sinful mind is hostile to God. It does not submit to God's law, nor can it do so. Those controlled by the sinful nature cannot please God." Check the correct responses:
❑ 1. The worldly mind is God's enemy.
❑ 2. The worldly mind is life and peace.
❑ 3. The worldly mind does not submit to God's law.
❑ 4. The worldly mind cannot please God.

God is not pleased with a mind that yields itself to sin. He considers it an enemy. It operates outside God's law. It brings the exact opposite of life and peace. The correct answers to the above exercise are 1, 3, and 4.

CHOOSING CHRIST DAILY

The spiritual Christian is not perfect. But daily this Christian crucifies the flesh and consciously allows the Spirit to fill him or her. When this person is tempted, he or she closes the door to Satan and opens the door to Jesus.

Read Romans 6:17-18: "Thanks be to God that, though you used to be slaves to sin, you wholeheartedly obeyed the form of teaching to which you were entrusted. You have been set free from sin and have become slaves to righteousness." Check the way a person who is a servant of sin can be made free from sin.
❑ 1. By obeying God's Word ❑ 2. By refusing to be tempted

Obeying God's Word is the way you can refrain from being a slave to sin. The Word contains everything you need for life and peace. It contains every instruction you need for living. You can recall the Word when you need a reminder of how you are to think and act. The correct answer is 1.

Memorizing Scripture helps you resist temptation. This week's Scripture-memory verses are Romans 6:12-13. Turn to page 114 and read them aloud. Then write how you think memorizing these verses will help you resist temptation.

___

___

You may have said that these verses remind you to use your body for good and not evil. Recalling them in a time of temptation can help you bind Satan and can remind you to ask God to help you.

IN THE CARPENTER'S SHOP

What are practical ways you can replace evil with good? Today look at another area of your life in which you want to be more Christlike.

Read the Scriptures in the margin that relate to greed. Underline the words or phrases related to greed. From the verses marked "The World's Way" identify a specific behavior you want to get rid of. From the verses marked "The Spirit's Way" identify an action you will take to replace it. I have given you an example. Each day this week you will record your progress in working on this behavior.

Here is an example.

Behavior I want to work on: overspending

An action I will take to put off the old self: no longer incur credit-card debt when I see an item I think I must purchase

An action I will take to let the Holy Spirit make me more like Christ: be content with what I have and control my material desires; memorize Hebrews 13:5 to help me do this

Now you try it.

Behavior I want to work on: ___

An action I will take to put off the old self:

___

An action I will take to let the Holy Spirit make me more like Christ:

___

The World's Way

"Among you there must not be even a hint of sexual immorality, or of any kind of impurity, or of greed, because these are improper for God's holy people" (Eph. 5:3).

"Put to death, therefore, whatever belongs to your earthly nature: sexual immorality, impurity, lust, evil desires and greed, which is idolatry" (Col. 3:5).

"The acts of the sinful nature are obvious: sexual immorality, impurity and debauchery. … I warn you, as I did before, that those who live like this will not inherit the kingdom of God" (Gal. 5:19-21).

The Spirit's Way

"Be imitators of God, therefore, as dearly loved children and live a life of love, just as Christ loved us and gave himself up for us as a fragrant offering and sacrifice to God" (Eph. 5:1-2).

"Set your minds on things above, not on earthly things" (Col. 3:2).

"The fruit of the Spirit is love, joy, peace, patience, kindness, goodness, faithfulness, gentleness, and self-control. Against such things there is no law" (Gal. 5:22-23).

Share with your prayer partner how the Holy Spirit helps you. Tell that person about the area you wish to change and ask him or her to pray with you that the Holy Spirit will help you set aside this behavior.

During your quiet time today read Ephesians 5, one of the chapters you have been reading for instructions on Christlike behaviors. Then complete the Daily Master Communication Guide on page 116.

DAY 2

Alert to the Enemy

Victorious living involves being aware of Satan's potential hold on you and keeping the enemy at a distance. Even though the human personality is God's highest creation, an individual's personality is damaged when he or she follows Satan and chooses to sin. Satan's weapons are powerful. Only a foolish Christian fails to take Satan seriously.

THE FORCES YOU FACE
Read the verses in the margin. Record the forces mentioned that are fighting against the Spirit of God within you.

"The sinful nature desires what is contrary to the Spirit, and the Spirit what is contrary to the sinful nature. They are in conflict with each other, so that you do not do what you want" (Gal. 5:17).

"Do not love the world or anything in the world. If anyone loves the world, the love of the Father is not in him" (1 John 2:15).

"Be self-controlled and alert. Your enemy the devil prowls around like a roaring lion looking for someone to devour" (1 Pet. 5:8).

Galatians 5:17: ______________________________

1 John 2:15: ______________________________

1 Peter 5:8: ______________________________

These verses make clear that the enemy is alive and vigilant in seeking to destroy Christians. He constantly looks for a weak point in your personality so that he can cause you to stumble. Your sinful nature, the world, and the devil are the forces that fight against the Spirit of God within you.

In each of the following case studies, underline the point at which Satan is fighting against the Spirit of God within the person.

Julie badly needed a job because she was the sole provider for herself and her son. Although she had taken courses to update her skills and had sought the help of an employment agency, she was still unemployed after a six-month search. Her bank account was drained, and her financial picture looked bleak. Julie, a

Christian, had trusted God with her job search but was beginning to doubt that God was aware of her distress.

Ken, a middle-aged father of three, was diagnosed with a life-threatening illness. At first he vowed that fighting this disease would not get him down, but the treatments and his discomfort were taking an emotional and physical toll. The time away from work because of the illness was endangering his job. Having served God faithfully as a Sunday School teacher for years, Ken wondered why God did not intervene.

Ray had worked diligently in his business and was successful. As his income increased, he acquired a larger home, a finer car, and numerous material possessions. Ray had always been active in his church, but his increased travel schedule, as well as his heightened interest in leisure activities, began taking more of his time. Soon he began to tell himself that he did not have time for church because he was such a busy, important person.

Satan attacked each individual at a point of weakness. When Julie questioned whether God was aware of her distress and when Ken questioned why God did not intervene in his suffering, they gave Satan an entry point in their lives. When Ray thought that he could make it on his own without the fellowship of other believers, he became vulnerable to the enemy.

Satan looks for moments of distress, doubt, fear, and pain to gain a foothold in your life. He sees these as golden opportunities to destroy your trust in God. The Holy Spirit can help you rest in the Lord and exercise self-control while you wait for God's help.

As you read the case studies, could you identify with any of them? Has Satan attempted to destroy you in a weak or anxious moment? If so, draw a star beside the illustration that is similar to the way you have been challenged. Identify a weak area of your life now or in the recent past. Briefly describe your struggle.

____

____

____

This week's Scripture-memory verses address the challenges you face when sin attempts to reign in your life. To continue your memory work, try to write Romans 6:12-13 in the blanks on the following page.

DAILY MASTER COMMUNICATION GUIDE

GALATIANS 5

What God said to me:

____

____

____

____

____

____

____

____

What I said to God:

____

____

____

____

____

____

____

____

____

____

____

____

THE VICTORY HAS BEEN WON
What has Jesus done to secure victory for you over the forces that fight against the Spirit of God within you? The three verses in the margin answer this question.

"What the law was powerless to do in that it was weakened by the sinful nature, God did by sending his own Son in the likeness of sinful man to be a sin offering. And so he condemned sin in sinful man" (Rom. 8:3).

" 'I have told you these things, so that in me you may have peace. In this world you will have trouble. But take heart! I have overcome the world' " (John 16:33).

"He who does what is sinful is of the devil, because the devil has been sinning from the beginning. The reason the Son of God appeared was to destroy the devil's work" (1 John 3:8).

Read the verses in the margin and describe what Jesus has done to conquer the enemy.

Romans 8:3: _______________

John 16:33: _______________

1 John 3:8: _______________

What a victory! You are not alone when you sustain Satan's attacks. Christ has gone before you to provide victory for you. In Christ's death on the cross He condemned sin in the flesh, He overcame the world, and He destroyed the devil's work. He has also given you the Holy Spirit to strengthen you in times of temptation.

Doesn't this marvelous news make you long for everyone you know to have this kind of power? Can you think of persons in your circles of influence who yield to temptation because they have never accepted Jesus? Perhaps you see them sinning as the devil takes control of them, and you long for them to know the One who has crushed Satan and has overcome the world.

Pray for two persons with whom you work or for two neighbors who do not know Jesus.

IN THE CARPENTER'S SHOP
How well are you withstanding Satan's attacks in your life? The Holy Spirit will help you put off a harmful thought or action and put on more Christlike character.

In day 1 you listed a behavior you hope to tear down to become more Christlike. Today describe an instance in which you have already begun to set aside that behavior.

____

____

During your quiet time today read Galatians 5, another chapter you have been reading for instructions on Christlike behavior. Then complete the Daily Master Communication Guide on page 119.

DAY 3

A Victory You Can Claim

Yesterday you learned that Jesus has already provided the victory for you when Satan tries to catch you at a weak moment and to turn your trust away from God. Picture the scene of Jesus dying on the cross for you. Do you know why He was there? So that you can participate in His victory over sin. Under the law no forgiveness of sins could occur without the shedding of blood. Jesus' death and resurrection make possible your righteousness before God. His sinless perfection is the only acceptable offering for your atonement. Without the shedding of Jesus' blood, no remission (removal) of sins could happen. Read Hebrews 9:22 in the margin.

"In fact, the law requires that nearly everything be cleansed with blood, and without the shedding of blood there is no forgiveness" (Heb. 9:22).

Read the verses in the margin that describe Jesus' victory over sin. Match each verse with the correct summary statement.

___ 1. Hebrews 9:26	**a. You are dead to sin through Jesus.**
___ 2. Romans 6:11	**b. Jesus' blood cleanses you from sin.**
___ 3. 1 Corinthians 15:56-57	**c. Jesus purified us from sin by His sacrifice.**
___ 4. 1 John 1:7	**d. You have victory over sin through Jesus.**

"Then Christ would have had to suffer many times since the creation of the world. But now he has appeared once for all at the end of the ages to do away with sin by the sacrifice of himself" (Heb. 9:26).

"Count yourselves dead to sin but alive to God in Christ Jesus" (Rom. 6:11).

"The sting of death is sin, and the power of sin is the law. But thanks be to God! He gives us the victory through our Lord Jesus Christ" (1 Cor. 15:56-57).

"If we walk in the light, as he is in the light, we have fellowship with one another, and the blood of Jesus, his Son, purifies us from all sin" (1 John 1:7).

The blood of our sinless Savior is the source of your cleansing from sin. It is as though you are dead to the power of sin. Sin is no longer your master. Jesus has provided a way out. The correct answers are 1. c, 2. a, 3. d, 4. b.

A LIFE OF VICTORY

Jesus' victory can be yours. Galatians 2:20 states two inseparable dynamics of victory: "I have been crucified with Christ and I no longer live, but Christ lives in me. The life I live in the body, I live by faith in the Son of God, who loved me and gave himself for me." One of those dynamics is death. The other is new life. One is repudiation of self-seeking and self-will. The other is complete commitment to Christ's lordship and God's will.

Daily Master Communication Guide

Colossians 3

What God said to me:

____

____

____

____

____

____

____

____

What I said to God:

____

____

____

____

____

____

____

____

____

Complete this verse with the words that describe these two dynamics in action. Check your work by looking in the previous paragraph.

"I have been ______________________ with Christ and

I no longer __________."

Death to a life of defeat at the hands of the world, the flesh, and the devil produces a life that is victorious over these three familiar foes. This theme is repeated in Romans 6:11, which appears in the margin on the previous page.

Read Romans 6:11 in the margin on the previous page. Write in your own words what this verse means.

____

____

Maybe you paraphrased the verse like this: I think of myself as dead to sin but alive through Jesus Christ.

The verse you paraphrased, Romans 6:11, appears in your Bible just before this week's Scripture-memory verses, Romans 6:12-13. Practice saying aloud your memory verses. Take this opportunity to review the other verses you have memorized in this study.

How do you feel about the fact that Jesus' victory over sin can be yours? Check the statement or statements that apply:

- ❑ **I have a difficult time believing that this is possible. Sin and the devil are too powerful to be overcome.**
- ❑ **I want to believe that I have victory over sin, but I feel unworthy.**
- ❑ **I don't deserve this kind of love, but I believe God's Word when it says that this is a precious gift to me, and I accept it freely.**
- ❑ **Other: ____**

____

Christ's victory over sin is a popular theme in sermons and lessons in churches. Using the Hearing the Word form on page 141, write what you learn from a Sunday School lesson or a sermon this week or in the next few weeks, especially on the topic of victorious living.

IN THE CARPENTER'S SHOP

How are you claiming Christ's victory in your efforts to put off the old self and to replace it with the new?

Yesterday you wrote about progress you are making in tearing down old habits in areas related to greed. Today describe something new Christ is adding to your life to replace the old.

____

____

During your quiet time today read Colossians 3, the third passage from which you have been receiving instruction about living a Christlike life. Let God speak to you through this passage. Then complete the Daily Master Communication Guide on page 122.

DAY 4

Resisting Temptation

Victory in Jesus Christ may seem easy enough to claim when you are listening to a good sermon at church or when you are having a meaningful quiet time at home. But what about when you are on the job, in a family conflict, or in a personal struggle? How do you experience victory in the heat of daily circumstances?

STRENGTH TO WITHSTAND TEMPTATION

To understand how to experience this victory, first study how sin takes root in your life. Sin begins with temptation. The Bible says that Jesus was tempted in every way you are tempted; yet He did not sin (see Heb. 4:15 in the margin). How reassuring it is to realize that He knows and understands when you find yourself on the verge of falling into Satan's snares. Because Jesus understands, He can help you when you are tempted (see Heb. 2:18 in the margin).

"We do not have a high priest who is unable to sympathize with our weaknesses, but we have one who has been tempted in every way, just as we are—yet was without sin" (Heb. 4:15).

"Because he himself suffered when he was tempted, he is able to help those who are being tempted" (Heb. 2:18).

"No temptation has seized you except what is common to man. And God is faithful; he will not let you be tempted beyond what you can bear. But when you are tempted, he will also provide a way out so that you can stand up under it" (1 Cor. 10:13).

Read 1 Corinthians 10:13 in the margin. Based on what you read, explain what is wrong with this statement: Some temptations are so strong that they cannot be resisted.

____

____

No temptation is too strong to withstand. For every temptation God provides a way of escape.

" 'Watch and pray so that you will not fall into temptation. The spirit is willing, but the body is weak' " (Matt. 26:41).

What impact does prayer have on temptation? Read Matthew 26:41 in the margin. Then check the correct answer.
❑ If you pray, you will not be tempted.
❑ Through prayer you can resist temptation.

The verse from Matthew that you read contains words spoken by Jesus when He was in the garden of Gethsemane with the disciples. He knew that they would need more than willing spirits to withstand the temptation ahead of them. He knew that they needed to be fortified with prayer. Prayer does not prevent temptation. Temptation will always occur. Prayer can give you the spiritual strength to resist temptation.

FLEEING TEMPTATION

Evil thoughts and desires may pass through a person's mind. That is temptation. Temptation itself is not sin. Dwelling on those thoughts—letting the mind entertain the idea—*is* sin. When a worldly Christian "window-shops" for sin, the devil comes to the door and invites the worldly Christian in. The worldly Christian responds, "Oh, no, just looking." Yet this person's openness to temptation often leads to sin.

"Flee the evil desires of youth, and pursue righteousness, faith, love and peace, along with those who call on the Lord out of a pure heart" (2 Tim. 2:22).

What does the Bible warn a spiritual Christian to do about temptation? Read 2 Timothy 2:22 in the margin. A spiritual Christian is warned to—
❑ run away from temptation;
❑ seek it.

What does the same verse say that a spiritual Christian is to follow?

____

____

A spiritual Christian is to follow righteousness, faith, love, and peace. If right living; faith in God; and loving, peaceful relationships are the goals, a spiritual Christian has an arsenal of weapons to use in times of temptation.

Reread the case studies on page 118–19. Describe the steps each Christian could take to withstand temptation.

Julie: ____

____

____

Ken: ____

____

____

Ray: ____

____

____

Julie is a prime candidate for Satan's attack because of her discouragement. She could resist Satan by admitting her frustration in her job hunt while remembering God's faithfulness to her in the past and seeking assurance from Scripture that He cares about His children. She could ask other Christians to give her other tips for finding a job. She could consider other sources of financial help if she feels that she is becoming destitute.

Resisting temptation during physical pain like Ken's takes strength of character that only the Holy Spirit makes possible. Ken could lay his physical condition and his future at the foot of the cross, believing that he can trust the days ahead to the God who created him and preserved him until this time. He could acknowledge his feelings of loneliness and helplessness. He could pray about his options, including other courses of treatment or other medical opinions. He could examine alternative ways of generating income for his family, such as working at home or working part-time, until his health improves.

Ray's arrogance and self-importance are ways Satan is gaining a foothold in his life. The Holy Spirit can convict Ray of sin in his life and can bring him to seek forgiveness. Ray could reexamine his use of time and resources. Besides returning to regular fellowship with believers, he could spend some of his leisuretime in ministry programs of the church. Instead of placing self-gratification at the center of his life, he could focus on Christ as his main priority.

"If we confess our sins, he is faithful and just and will forgive us our sins and purify us from all unrighteousness. If we claim we have not sinned, we make him out to be a liar and his word has no place in our lives" (1 John 1:9-10).

Everyone, even a spiritual person, sins. What should you do when the Holy Spirit convicts you of sin in your life? Read 1 John 1:9-10 in the margin and write *true* beside the correct statement:

_________ **1. You should say that you have not sinned.**

_________ **2. You should confess your sin.**

_________ **3. You should punish yourself for your sin.**

DAILY MASTER COMMUNICATION GUIDE

JOB 1

What God said to me:

____

____

____

____

____

____

____

____

What I said to God:

____

____

____

____

____

____

____

____

____

No one is above sin. God wants you to confess sin. Confession enables God to keep His promise to forgive you. The correct statement is 2.

Whom do you know who needs to hear the healing message that God forgives sin? Many persons within your circles of influence live in the bondage of sin, not knowing that they can claim God's promise to wipe away their sins. Your testimony can help you share that good news.

Continue to work on your testimony, using the ideas your leader gave you last week. Remember to limit it to three minutes. Be ready to give your testimony at the Testimony Workshop that follows this study.

What do this week's Scripture-memory verses say that you are to do about the sin in your life?

____

____

Say aloud this week's Scripture-memory verses. Then review the verses you memorized during the previous weeks of this study.

During your quiet time today read Job 1, which describes Job's refusal to sin in the face of discouragement. See how God speaks to you through this passage. Then complete the Daily Master Communication Guide in the margin.

APPLYING THE DISCIPLE'S PERSONALITY

Practice explaining in your own words how to apply the Disciple's Personality, using Galatians 5:16-25. Your leader should have explained how to do this in your previous group session. On the basic diagram on the following page, close the door of the flesh as you draw a cross in the center of the circle to encompass *spirit, flesh, mind, will,* and *emotions.* Write *crucified* across *flesh.* Now write *walk, led,* and *live* above the circle and draw an arrow above these words pointing up. Write *fruit of the Spirit* above the arrow and draw above these words another upward arrow pointing to *God.* Then write *lusts* and *desires* below the circle with an arrow pointing down toward *works of the flesh.* Draw another arrow that points down toward *Satan.* See page 140 if you need help with your drawing.

GOD

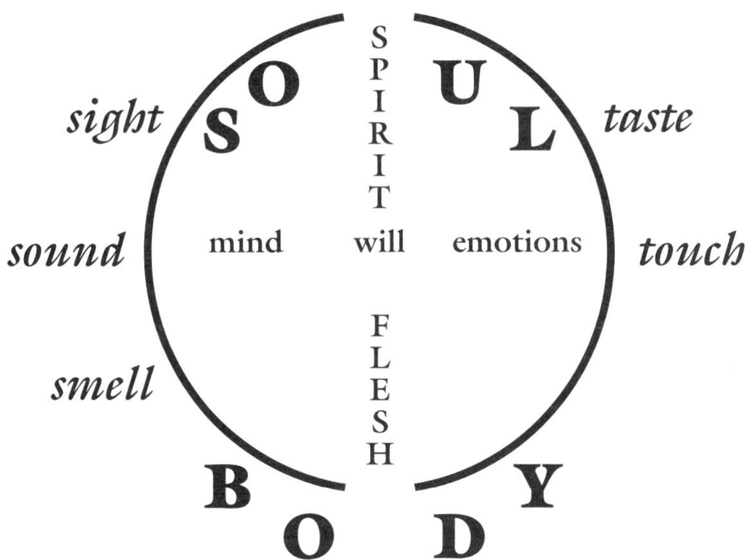

SATAN

Now write your explanation here.

DAY 5

Victory in Jesus

Once as I returned on a flight from a speaking engagement, a young woman who attended the conference sat down next to my wife and me and told one of the most amazing stories about victorious living that I have ever heard. She now lets her light shine in a country that allows little access to the gospel, but she described a life that began anything but victoriously.

The young woman was one of six children of an alcoholic father. By the age of 13 she was living on the street on her own. From there her life spiraled downward. Yet through determination she went to college, got a degree in elementary education, and started teaching. She noticed that one of her students, a nine-year-old girl, seemed different. After school she helped erase the chalkboard and clean the room, and the two became good friends. One day the student asked the woman if she went to church. The woman answered that she used to go to confession with her mother. The girl asked her teacher to help her learn Scripture verses she needed to learn before being baptized. The first Scripture was John 3:16. When the woman read it, she cried. "I couldn't imagine that God loved me after what I had done," the woman recalled.

The woman then attended a church service and cried all the way through it. "I talked to my live-in boyfriend and told him that we needed to change," she said. One day when he was away, she returned home to find a man ransacking her apartment in search of money. When she could give him no money, he raped her. The woman recounted what happened next: "After it was over, I opened the Bible to John 3:16, which was the only verse I knew. Then he said that he knew what he had done was wrong but that his mother was sick and needed money. He asked me to forgive him. I responded, 'If God is willing to forgive me for all I've done, how can I refuse to forgive you?' We knelt, and he asked for forgiveness. Asking forgiveness for my sinful lifestyle, I turned over my life to Christ. Two weeks later I went back to church and made my profession of faith. My boyfriend would not change, so I moved out."

"If God is willing to forgive me for all I've done, how can I refuse to forgive you?"

The woman then began praying for her parents' salvation. Six years later, they gave their lives to Christ. She began serving at church, then went on mission trips to Mexico and Belize. Now she serves as a missionary. She concluded her story: "I praise God for His goodness and His love. I am thankful that I can show His love to people who don't know anything about Him."

As she returned to her seat on the plane, I said to myself: "O the depth of riches both of the wisdom and knowledge of God! How unsearchable are His … ways" (Rom. 11:33, KJV). After I heard the way Christ had graciously forgiven her and had helped her become a fervent, bright witness for Him, I understood even more clearly the victory we have in Christ.

Because of the cross, God forgives and accepts you, just like the woman on the plane. Therefore, you have no need to try to make things right yourself or to give up in despair. From the cross Jesus gives you His righteousness as you are crucified and resurrected with Him.

Jesus assures His disciples that those who suffer with Him will someday reign with him (see 2 Tim. 2:11-13 in the margin). His victory points to the future, but it is also present tense.

"If we died with him,
we will also live with him;
If we endure,
we will also reign with him.
if we disown him,
he will also disown us;
if we are faithless,
he will remain faithful,
for he cannot disown himself"
(2 Tim. 2:11-13).

IN THE CARPENTER'S SHOP

How has the Holy Spirit been working in you this week to build Christlike character? How are you progressing in getting rid of the old self and in letting the Spirit add new behaviors to your life?

Complete the following as you think about the changes related to greed that you identified earlier this week.

Something I have been getting rid of this week:

____

Something Christ has been adding to my character this week:

____

Stop and thank God for the gift of the Holy Spirit to help mold you into Christlikeness.

Meditate on the moral and spiritual victories Jesus has won for you during the past few weeks. Identify areas of your life in which you are still suffering defeat.

____

____

Review the seven steps to Christlike character listed at the end of the Disciple's Personality presentation (p. 139). What steps do you need to take to achieve victory in every area of your life?

____

____

____

APPLYING THE DISCIPLE'S PERSONALITY

Now that you are approaching the end of *MasterLife 2: The Disciple's Personality*, you are asked to demonstrate your knowledge of the Disciple's Personality, which you have been learning throughout this study. Draw and explain in your own words the Disciple's Personality to another group member. Say the verses that go with it. See pages 133–39 if you need help.

I hope that you have found worthwhile your Scripture memorization during this study. You have memorized six Scriptures that accompany various aspects of the Disciple's Personality. Nothing you have done in this study has been without an investment of time. I hope that this process has helped you hide God's Word in your heart so that you can use it, along with the concepts of the Disciple's Personality, in a variety of situations.

Write the verses you have memorized during this study. See how well you can remember them without looking back. Be prepared to say them to a partner at the Testimony Workshop at the end of this study.

Romans 6:12-13: ______________________________

____

Ephesians 5:18: ______________________________

____

Philippians 2:13: ______________________________

____

Romans 12:1-2: ______________________________

____

Galatians 5:22-23: ______________________________

____

1 Corinthians 6:19-20: ______________________________

____

THE TESTIMONY WORKSHOP

As you have participated in this study, you have learned essential elements for writing your Christian testimony, which you should be ready to present at the Testimony Workshop that follows this study. I hope that this will be a meaningful experience for you.

Practice giving your testimony to others as you prepare to present it during the Testimony Workshop at the conclusion of this study. Remember to limit it to three minutes. Be prepared to present it in a variety of situations—to a skeptical person, to someone who is eager to hear, to someone who believes that he or she can earn salvation, and so on.

During your quiet time today read 2 Timothy 2, in which Paul instructed Timothy about claiming victory in Christ. Then complete the Daily Master Communication Guide in the margin.

HAS THIS WEEK MADE A DIFFERENCE?

Review "My Walk with the Master This Week" at the beginning of this week's material. Mark the activities you have finished by drawing vertical lines in the diamonds beside them. Finish any incomplete activities.

Congratulations on completing your study of *MasterLife 2: The Disciple's Personality.* I hope that the concept of life in the Spirit has new meaning for you after these six weeks of study. Examining the warring components of your personality is challenging, often requiring that you admit your weaknesses and temptations even though you like to think of yourself as someone who does not easily stumble. I pray that this process has made you more aware of the vulnerable areas of your life so that you can be more alert to times when you need to close the door of the flesh. May the Holy Spirit strengthen you as you claim victory in Christ.

What a great time of fellowship and growth you have to look forward to when you attend the Testimony Workshop! By now your leader has probably given you details about this workshop. I predict that you will be moved in ways you cannot imagine when you hear reports of ways the Holy Spirit has worked in group members' lives. Most importantly, you will be empowered and motivated as you refine and polish your own three-minute testimony and prepare to share it with persons who need to hear it. The workshop will give you strength and courage to bear witness that you never thought you could experience. Furthermore, you will receive an exciting preview of *MasterLife 3: The Disciple's Victory*, which I hope you are planning to study next. You have great days ahead as a disciple of Jesus Christ!

Daily Master Communication Guide

2 Timothy 2

What God said to me:

____

____

____

____

____

____

____

____

What I said to God:

____

____

____

____

____

____

____

____

____

The Disciple's Cross

The Disciple's Cross provides an instrument for visualizing and understanding your opportunities and responsibilities as a disciple of Christ. It depicts the six biblical disciplines of a balanced Christian life. *MasterLife 1: The Disciple's Cross* interprets the biblical meanings of the disciplines and illustrates in detail how to draw and present the Disciple's Cross.

Because *MasterLife 2: The Disciple's Personality* refers to elements of the Disciple's Cross and your weekly work includes assignments related to the six disciplines, a brief overview of the Disciple's Cross is provided here.

As a disciple of Jesus Christ, you have—

1 Lord as the first priority of your life;

2 relationships: a vertical relationship with God and horizontal relationships with others;

3 commitments: deny self, take up your cross daily, and follow Christ;

4 resources to center your life in Christ: the Word, prayer, fellowship, and witness;

5 ministries that grow from the four resources: teaching/preaching, worship/intercession, nurture, evangelism, and service;

6 disciplines of a disciple: spend time with the Master, live in the Word, pray in faith, fellowship with believers, witness to the world, and minister to others. By practicing these biblical principles, you can abide in Christ and can be useful in the Master's service.

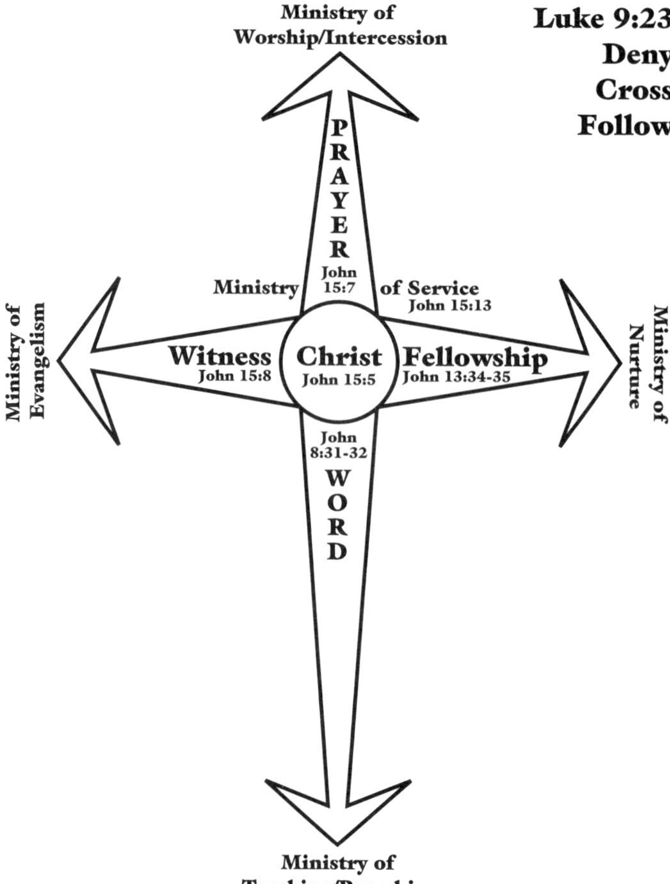

The Disciple's Personality

The Disciple's Personality is the focal point for all you learn in *MasterLife 2: The Disciple's Personality*. This presentation provides an instrument for understanding why you think, feel, and act as you do and explains how to become more Christlike in character and behavior.

Following are step-by-step instructions for presenting the Disciple's Personality to another person. Each week of this study you learn an additional portion of the presentation and the Scripture that accompanies it. As you learn the Disciple's Personality and review it in the future, you may find it helpful to refer to this step-by-step explanation and to the drawings. Do not attempt to memorize this presentation. You will learn how to present it in your own words. Do not feel overwhelmed by the amount of material involved. You will learn it in weekly segments. By the end of the study you will be able to explain the entire Disciple's Personality and to say all of the verses that accompany it.

To explain the Disciple's Personality to someone, use blank, unlined sheets of paper to draw the illustrations shown. Instructions to you are in parentheses. The material that follows is the presentation you make to the other person. The words in **bold type** indicate when to add to your drawings.

Perhaps you sometimes wonder why you think, feel, and act as you do. May I draw an illustration that helped me understand myself? This drawing illustrates biblical teachings about your personality. It shows you how to make Christ Master of your life and how to master life.

A UNIFIED PERSONALITY

(Draw an incomplete circle in the center of a blank sheet of paper, leaving spaces at the top and the bottom of the circle as shown below. Write the word *God* above the circle.) **God** created you as a physical and spiritual being. The physical part came from the earth. The spiritual part originated in God's Spirit. The circle represents you—your total personality. The Bible describes you as a unity. That's why I drew one circle to represent your personality. I will add each element of your personality as I explain it. When you understand each element of your personality and how it functions, you will discover how to integrate your personality under the lordship of Christ.

Body

(Write *body* beneath the circle. Write the five senses on each side of the circle as illustrated below.) The Bible

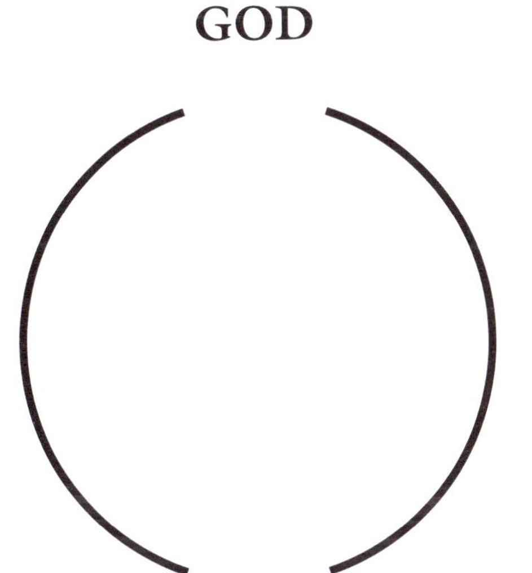

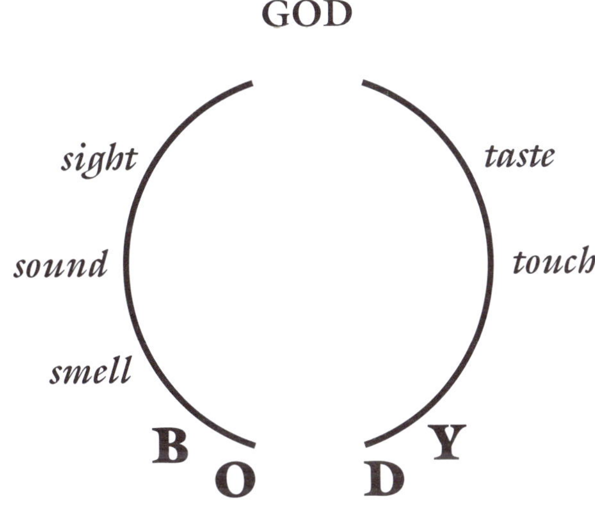

pictures you as a **body.** God made your body from the earth to serve several functions. Through your body you are able to participate in the physical world. Your **five senses** relate you to the rest of God's creation. Your body makes it possible to communicate with the world around you and with other living creatures. Your body gives you a physical identity that makes you a distinct, unique personality. God created your body good.

Soul

(Write the word *soul* inside the circle as illustrated. Write the words *mind, will,* and *emotions* as illustrated. Write the word *spirit* as illustrated below.) The Bible also pictures you as a **soul.** You do not just have a soul; you *are* a soul. Genesis 2:7 says that the first human being became a living soul when God breathed into his nostrils the breath of life. God imparted His life to the

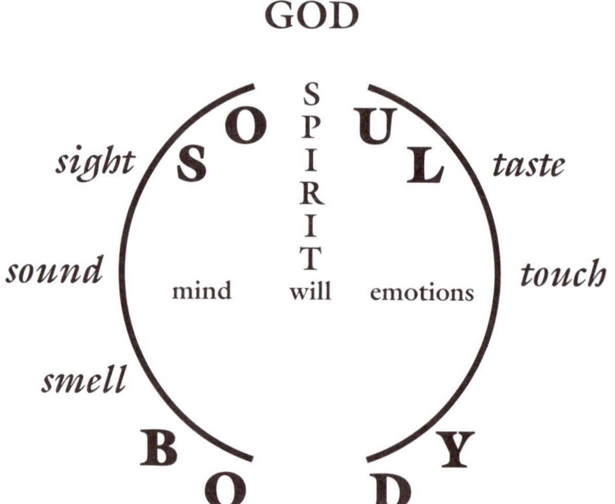

person He had made. The words for *soul* in the Bible generally mean *life* or *the total self*. When the Bible says that a person's soul is saved or lost, it refers to the total person. Sometimes the word for *soul* means *heart* or *the seat of the will, desires, and affection—the inner human being*. The word *psyche* originates from the Greek word for *soul*. The soul's ability to think, will, and feel provides additional evidence that human beings are created in the image of God. These three elements—**mind, will, and emotions**—help form your distinctive personality.

Spirit

The Bible also pictures you as **spirit.** Your spirit directly relates you to God's image. It gives you the capacity to be aware of yourself and to fellowship and work with God. People and God are able to communicate directly. When God finished creating the first person, Genesis 1:31 says, "It was very good."[1]

THE NATURAL PERSON

The Flesh

(Write *Satan* beneath the circle.) Soon after the creation another spiritual being entered God's good creation. Humanity succumbed to **Satan**'s temptation and disobeyed God. A different aspect of the spiritual nature entered the personality of human beings. That aspect is called the flesh. The Bible uses the word *flesh* in two ways. The general meaning is *body*, referring to the physical body. The other meaning is symbolic, referring to the lower nature. It refers to the human capacity to sin and to follow Satan instead of God.

(Draw two open doors on the inside of the circle. Draw a handle inside each door.) Notice that the illustration has two doors. The top door, **the door of the spirit,** allows you to relate to God. The bottom door, **the door of the flesh,** allows you to relate to Satan. God created human beings with free will. Notice that the will stands between the door of the spirit and the door of the flesh and that the door handles are on the

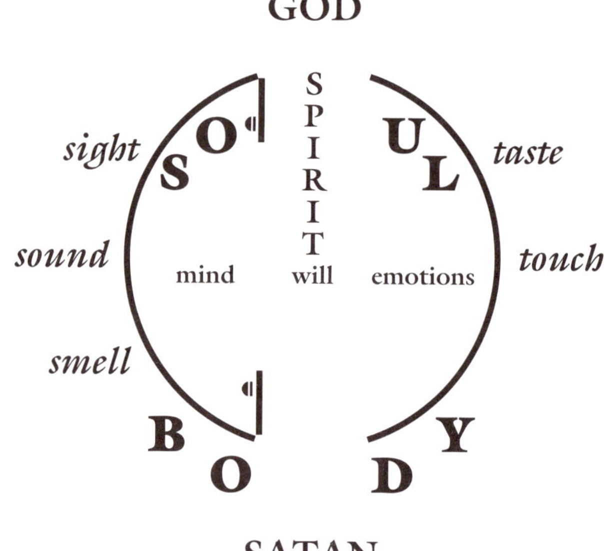

inside. Unfortunately, when Adam and Eve, the first human beings, were tempted by Satan, they chose to turn from God's leading to follow Satan's leading. At that moment the human being's ego, the big ***I***, took over. (Draw lines between the two doors to form an *I* as illustrated below. Close the door of the spirit by completing the circle at the top. Draw a line through the word *spirit* as shown. Write *flesh* as illustrated. Leave the door of the flesh open.) The door of the **spirit** closed, and humanity died spiritually. The door of the **flesh** opened, and the sinful nature became the spiritual part of human personality. The results were terrible. The flesh came alive, causing the mind, will, and emotions to degenerate. The entire personality—body, soul, and spirit—was infiltrated by evil and death.

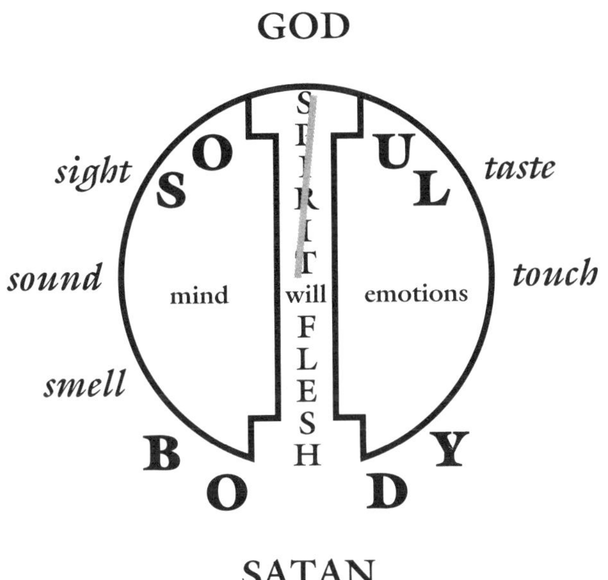

Through Satan's temptation humanity transgressed God's command and fell from its original innocence. Consequently, the descendants of the first sinful human beings inherit a nature and an environment inclined toward sin. As soon as they are capable of moral action, they become transgressors and are responsible to God for closing the door of the spirit and for shutting Him out.

The Condition of the Natural Person Today

(Write *The Natural Person* and *1 Corinthians 2:14* above the drawing.) **The natural person** is centered in himself or herself and is open to Satan's temptation and power. This person is unable to relate to God properly. **First Corinthians 2:14** says, "The man without the Spirit does not accept the things that come from the Spirit of God, for they are foolishness to him, and he cannot understand them, because they are spiritually discerned."

Your thoughts are influenced by evil; your emotions control you; your will is weak. Even strong-willed and disciplined persons are not able to overcome the effects of the flesh. No matter how many good things you do, the Bible says that a natural person cannot please God. People can come to God only as the Holy Spirit draws them.

The Natural Person

1 Cor. 2:14

GOD

S O U L
sight
sound
smell
taste
touch
mind
will
emotions
SPIRIT
FLESH
B O D Y

SATAN

God loves you even though you have sinned. He sent His only Son to pay for your sins so that you would not perish but have eternal life. Jesus died on the cross to save you from sin and death and to bring you to God. After His resurrection He sent the Holy Spirit to earth to draw you to God.

The Holy Spirit can speak to a natural person even though the door of the spirit is closed. When you open the door of the spirit, the Spirit of God enters your personality, and your spirit is born again.

(If you are using this illustration with a lost person, move directly to the section "The Spiritual Christian." If you are talking with a Christian, proceed with "The Worldly Christian.")

THE WORLDLY CHRISTIAN

(Draw the illustration shown below. It is the same as the previous one without the line through *spirit* and with both doors left open. Write *The Worldly Christian* and *1 Corinthians 3:1-3* above the diagram.) Now I will draw the same **circle** to illustrate the worldly Christian. This person has **opened the door of the spirit** but has also **left open the door of flesh**. This person still lives in the flesh even though he or she has

The Worldly Christian

1 Cor. 3:1-3

GOD

sight
S O
U L
taste
sound
mind
SPIRIT
will
FLESH
emotions
touch
smell
B O
D Y

SATAN

been born again. At some point this person realized that Christ could give him or her eternal life. This person opened the door of the spirit and was born again by the power of the Holy Spirit. This Christian was

made alive and became a partaker of the divine nature but failed to grow as he or she should.

Second Peter 1:3-4 says: "His divine power has given us everything we need for life and godliness through our knowledge of him who called us by his own glory and goodness. Through these he has given us his very great and precious promises, so that through them you may participate in the divine nature and escape the corruption in the world caused by evil desires." This passage then lists character traits a Christian needs to add as he or she grows: "Make every effort to add to your faith goodness; and to goodness, knowledge; and to knowledge, self-control; and to self-control, perseverance; and to perseverance, godliness; and to godliness, brotherly kindness; and to brotherly kindness, love" (2 Pet. 1:5-7). If the person does not do this, he or she will be ineffective, unproductive, nearsighted, and blind. The person will have "forgotten that he has been cleansed from his past sins" (2 Pet. 1:9). These characteristics describe the worldly Christian. Christians who are not taught how to grow and live in the Spirit remain as they were when they were born again. They are still babies in the faith, although they may have been believers for many years. **First Corinthians 3:1-3** describes this person's immature spiritual life: "Brothers, I could not address you as spiritual but as worldly—mere infants in Christ. I gave you milk, not solid food, for you were not yet ready for it. Indeed, you are still not ready. You are still worldly."

(Trace over the letter *s* with a capital *S* as shown below.) I will trace over the letter *s* in *spirit* with a **capital** *S* to show that the Holy Spirit is eternally a part of your spirit when you are born again. The worldly Christian's big mistake is having left open the door of the flesh. Satan still has access to this person, because the flesh dominates his or her thoughts, will, and emotions. The word *worldly* means *fleshly* or *carnal*. This type of Christian is more likely to follow the physical senses and fallen nature than the spiritual nature he or she received at conversion.

The Worldly Christian

1 Cor. 3:1-3

GOD

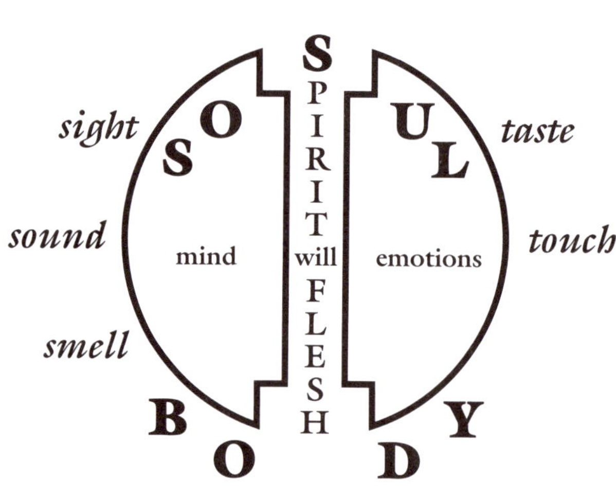

SATAN

No doubt you sometimes feel conflict in your heart when you try to have the thoughts, attitudes, and actions of Jesus. Why does such conflict arise? If you do not allow Christ continually to be the Master of your life through His Spirit, you are a worldly Christian. Although you have allowed Christ to enter your life, you still struggle to control your own life. The big *I* of the old, natural person still dominates you. Worldly Christians continually open the door of the flesh, allowing the old nature to determine what they think, do, and feel, rather than follow the Spirit of God.

Competing influences cause this conflict in your personality. You hear Satan's voice through your flesh, and you hear God's voice as His Spirit speaks to your spirit. You hear the voice of self through your mind, will, and emotions. You become a battleground. How can you have victory in this kind of situation? Do not despair. Christ wants to be your Lord and to give you daily victory.

THE SPIRITUAL CHRISTIAN

(Draw another circle with the labels you used previously. Add the cross in the center as shown below. Leave the door of the spirit open and close the door of the flesh. Write *The Spiritual Christian* and *Galatians 2:20* above the circle as illustrated. Write *crucified* across *flesh.*) I will draw the **circle** once more to illustrate the spiritual Christian. As Christ's disciple, you are promised victory over the world, the flesh, and the devil. Here is how. Notice that your **will** is located between **the door of the spirit** and **the door of the flesh**. The door of the spirit is open, while the door of the flesh is closed. When you are willing to let Christ master your life, His death on the cross and His resurrection give you a life of victory. You can say, as the apostle Paul did in **Galatians 2:20:** "I have been crucified with Christ and I no longer live, but Christ lives in me. The life I live in the body, I live by faith in the Son of God, who loved me and gave himself for me."

The way to have victory is to consider your flesh **crucified.** Because this is an ongoing act of your will, the indwelling Christ helps you keep the door of the spirit open and the door of the flesh closed. As you put your old self to death, the Spirit of God gives you life daily to live in victory. When you do this, you are filled with the Spirit of God. You are able to live in the Spirit. God takes control of your mind, your will, your emotions, and therefore your soul and body.

Now you can see the contrast between the natural person and the worldly Christian. You can also see that the **spiritual Christian** walks in the Spirit so that he or she will not yield to the desires of the flesh.

STEPS TO VICTORIOUS LIVING

(Write *Philippians 2:13* under *will.* Write *Ephesians 5:18* above *Spirit.* Write *Romans 12:2* under *mind.* Write *Galatians 5:22-23* under *emotions.* Write *Romans 6:12-13* under *flesh.* Read or quote these

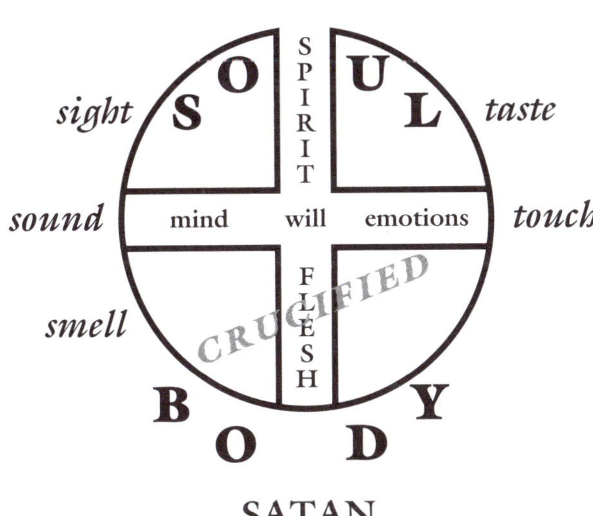

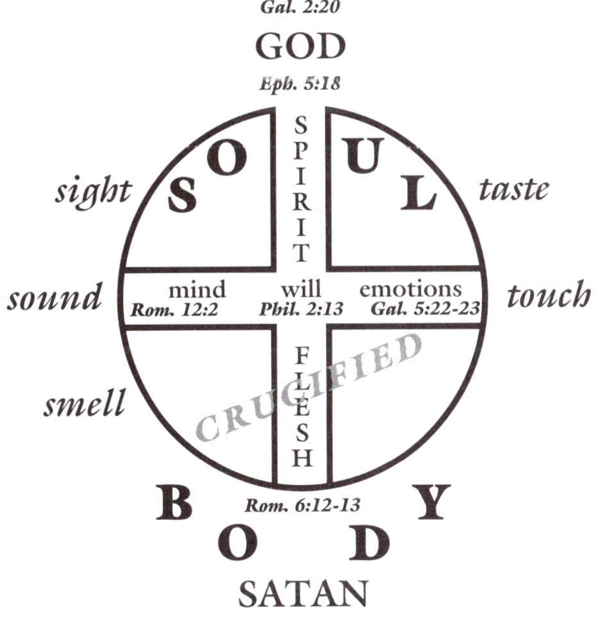

Scriptures as you write.) Your victory is not automatic. As long as you live in your body, you continually fight the good fight of faith. But God promises you victory. Let me explain in practical terms how to let Christ master your total personality and how to let Him enable you to live in the Spirit.

Philippians 2:13 says, "It is God who works in you to will and to act according to his good purpose." God helps you want to do His will and then gives you the ability to do it. By an act of your will, claim Galatians 2:20 as your own experience.

Ephesians 5:18 says, "Be filled with the Spirit." Ask the Holy Spirit to fill your personality and to keep filling you so that He can guide you, teach you, and give you the power to be a spiritual person.

Romans 12:2 says: "Do not conform any longer to the pattern of this world, but be transformed by the renewing of your mind. Then you will be able to test and approve what God's will is—his good, pleasing and perfect will."

Galatians 5:22-23 says: "The fruit of the Spirit is love, joy, peace, patience, kindness, goodness, faithfulness, gentleness and self-control. Against such things there is no law." As you allow the Spirit of God to fill you, He produces in you the fruit of the Spirit. The fruit of the Spirit helps produce the right emotions in you and helps you control your emotions.

Romans 6:12-13 says: "Do not let sin reign in your mortal body so that you obey its evil desires. Do not offer the parts of your body to sin, as instruments of wickedness, but rather offer yourselves to God, as those who have been brought from death to life; and offer the parts of your body to him as instruments of righteousness." Your body is God's gift to you so that you can have an identity, participate in this world, and communicate with others. It is not evil in itself; only the flesh or your sinful nature is evil. Jesus came to live in your body to make it an instrument of righteousness instead of an instrument of sin. Present your body and all of its members to God to do good.

(Write *1 Corinthians 6:19-20* on one side of the circle and *Romans 12:1* on the other side of the circle.) The idea of punishing the body because it is evil is not a Christian idea. **First Corinthians 6:19-20** says: "Do you not know that your body is a temple of the Holy Spirit, who is in you, whom you have received from God? You are not your own; you were bought at a

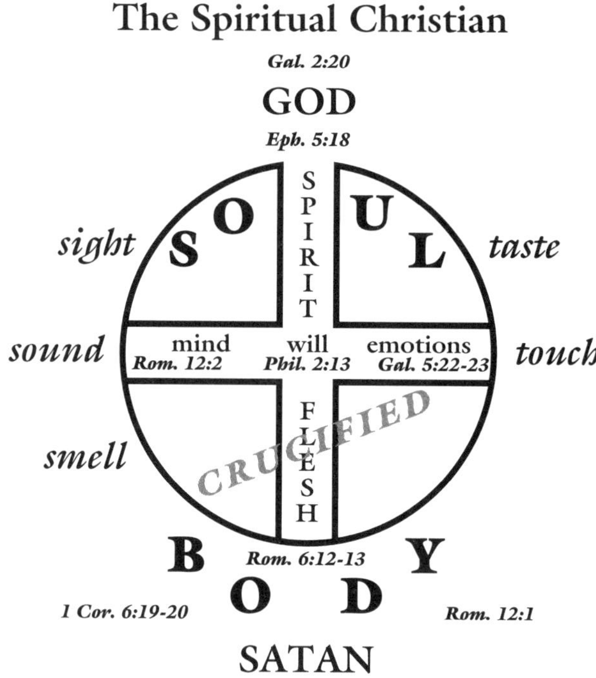

price. Therefore honor God with your body." **Romans 12:1** says, "I urge you, brothers, in view of God's mercy, to offer your bodies as living sacrifices, holy and pleasing to God—this is your spiritual act of worship." Christ's incarnation in a human body shows its potential for being restored to its original condition when Christ returns again and gives you a spiritual body like His.

As you fully yield yourself to God, the Holy Spirit helps you master your mind, your will, your emotions, your body, and your soul through the power of Christ. The life you live now, you live "by faith in the Son of God," as Galatians 2:20 says. As you obey Christ and His commands, He lives in you and you in Him. Christ lives in the world through you. Your inner self is integrated, and you experience peace. You are continually being filled with the Holy Spirit, and you overflow with joy, love, peace, praise, and thanksgiving. Rivers of living water flow from you to other persons as a witness to Christ, who lives in you through the Spirit.

WHO ARE YOU?

Now evaluate your life.

- Are you a natural person whose spirit is dead? Do your bodily senses and your natural desires control you?
- Are you a worldly Christian who has allowed Christ to enter your life but is still being mastered

by the desires of the flesh? Is the big *I* still in control?

- Are you a spiritual Christian who has been crucified with Christ and is being controlled by the Holy Spirit?

(Write *1 Thessalonians 5:23-24* under *Galatians 2:20.)* **First Thessalonians 5:23-24** says: "May God himself, the God of peace, sanctify you through and through. May your whole spirit, soul and body be kept blameless at the coming of our Lord Jesus Christ. The one who calls you is faithful and he will do it."

Spiritual Christians are not perfect, but daily they crucify the flesh and consciously allow the Holy Spirit to fill them. When they are tempted, they invite Christ to fill their lives, and they close the door of the flesh. When they sin, they ask for God's forgiveness and strength to help them overcome the next temptation.

The Spiritual Christian

Gal. 2:20
1 Thess. 5:23-24
GOD
Eph. 5:18
SPIRIT
SOUL
sight
taste
sound
touch
smell
mind *Rom. 12:2*
will *Phil. 2:13*
emotions *Gal. 5:22-23*
FLESH
CRUCIFIED
Rom. 6:12-13
BODY
1 Cor. 6:19-20
Rom. 12:1
SATAN

Remember these seven steps to Christlike character:

1. Ask God, through the Holy Spirit's guidance, to help you *will* to do the right thing.
2. Open the door of the *spirit* to the Spirit of God by asking Him to fill you.
3. Close the door of the *flesh* to Satan by confessing your sins and by claiming Christ's crucifixion of the flesh.
4. Renew your *mind* by saturating it with the Word of God.
5. Allow the Holy Spirit to master your *emotions* by producing the fruit of the Spirit in you.
6. Present your *body* to Christ as an instrument of righteousness.
7. Love the Lord your God with all your *heart,* with all your *soul,* with all your *mind,* and with all your *strength.*

---

[1]Some people believe that the soul and the spirit are the same rather than two distinct aspects of your personality. Their function is the same whether you think of your soul as having three parts (body, soul, and spirit) or two parts (body and soul, with the spirit being seen as the part of the soul). Although people who hold to each position believe they have a biblical basis for their position, your view of this matter does not affect the meaning of this presentation. It deals with the battle between the flesh and the spirit, not between the soul and the spirit.

Applying the Disciple's Personality

James 4:1-8

GOD
Draw near to God ↑ submit ↓ God will draw near to you
SOUL
SPIRIT
sight *taste*
sound mind will emotions *touch*
smell
FLESH
CRUCIFIED
BODY
resist
SATAN
will flee from you

Galatians 5:16-25

GOD
↑
FRUIT OF THE SPIRIT
↑
WALK
LED
LIVE
SOUL
SPIRIT
sight *taste*
sound mind will emotions *touch*
smell
FLESH
CRUCIFIED
BODY
LUSTS
DESIRES
↓
WORKS OF THE FLESH
↓
SATAN

Hearing the Word

Date ____________ **Place** ____________________

Speaker ______________ **Text** __________________

Title ______________________________________

Message
Points, explanation, illustrations, application:

Summary

The main thing the speaker wants me to do, be, and/or feel as a result of this message:

Application to My Life

What did God say to me through this message?

How does my life measure up to this word?

What action(s) will I take to bring my life in line with this word?

What truth do I need to study further?

Prayer-Covenant List

Request	Date	Bible Promise	Answer	Date

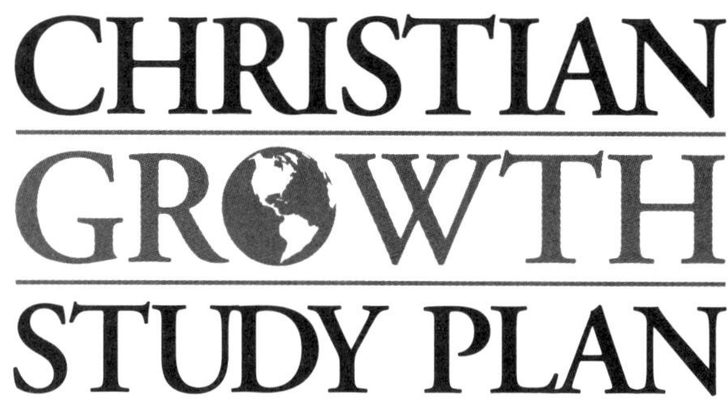

In the **Christian Growth Study Plan (formerly the Church Study Course)** *MasterLife 2: The Disciple's Personality* is a resource for course credit in the subject area Personal Life in the Christian Growth category of diploma plans. To receive credit, read the book; complete the learning activities; attend group sessions; show your work to your pastor, a staff member, or a church leader; and complete the following information. This page may be duplicated. Send the completed page to:

Christian Growth Study Plan
One LifeWay Plaza
Nashville, TN 37234-0117
Fax: (615)251-5067; email: ***cgspnet@lifeway.com***

For information about the Christian Growth Study Plan, refer to the Christian Growth Study Plan Catalog. It is located online at *www.lifeway.com/cgsp.* If you do not have access to the Internet, contact the Christian Growth Study Plan office (1.800.968.5519) for the specific plan you need for your ministry.

MasterLife 2: The Disciple's Personality
COURSE NUMBER: CG-0169

PARTICIPANT INFORMATION

Social Security Number (USA ONLY-optional)	Personal CGSP Number*	Date of Birth (MONTH, DAY, YEAR)
– –	– –	– –

Name (First, Middle, Last)	Home Phone
	– –

Address (Street, Route, or P.O. Box)	City, State, or Province	Zip/Postal Code

Please check appropriate box: ❑ Resource purchased by self ❑ Resource purchased by church ❑ Other

CHURCH INFORMATION

Church Name		
Address (Street, Route, or P.O. Box)	**City, State, or Province**	**Zip/Postal Code**

CHANGE REQUEST ONLY

☐ Former Name		
☐ Former Address	City, State, or Province	Zip/Postal Code
☐ Former Church	City, State, or Province	Zip/Postal Code

Signature of Pastor, Conference Leader, or Other Church Leader	Date

*New participants are requested but not required to give SS# and date of birth. Existing participants, please give CGSP# when using SS# for the first time. Thereafter, only one ID# is required. **Mail to:** Christian Growth Study Plan, One LifeWay Plaza, Nashville, TN 37234-0117. Fax: (615)251-5067.

Rev. 3-03